Editorial Project Manager

Eric Migliaccio

Editor in Chief

Karen J. Goldfluss, M.S. Ed.

Creative Director

Sarah M. Fournier

Cover Artist

Diem Pascarella

Illustrator

Clint McKnight

Art Coordinator

Renée Mc Elwee

Imaging

Amanda R. Harter

Publisher

Mary D. Smith, M.S. Ed.

MASTERING COMPLEX TEXT
Grade 4

TCR 8062

Using Multiple Reading Sources

Includes:

- 28 Units with 3 – 5 related text sources in a variety of genres and formats
- Multiple question types that promote higher-order thinking skills
- Open-ended response opportunities to encourage close reading
- Correlated to the Common Core State Standards

Teacher Created Resources

Author

Karen McRae

CORRELATED TO COMMON CORE STANDARDS

For correlations to the Common Core State Standards, see pages 109–112 of this book or visit *http://www.teachercreated.com/standards/*.

Teacher Created Resources

6421 Industry Way
Westminster, CA 92683
www.teachercreated.com

ISBN: 978-1-4206-8062-1

© 2015 Teacher Created Resources
Made in U.S.A.

Teacher Created Resources

Table of Contents

Introduction

Here we are, teaching and learning at the beginning of a new era of educational standards: the Common Core Era. This new directive has ushered in a slew of educational guidelines that are somewhat familiar and yet entirely ambitious. While the Common Core State Standards for English Language Arts address many educational basics (reading comprehension, proficiency in the conventions of English grammar, the ability to express oneself both in writing and in speech), they also seek to define what it means to be a literate, resourceful, perceptive person in the 21st century. Ultimately, they aim to equip each student with the tools needed to be that kind of person.

Introduction (cont.)

With this new, ambitious focus comes the need for a new type of educational material—one that challenges and interests students while meeting the multifaceted criteria of the Common Core. There are a total of 28 units in *Mastering Complex Text Using Multiple Reading Sources*, and each one fits the bill. Here's how:

✳ **The units in this book are both familiar and innovative.**

They are familiar in that they pair reading passages with activities that test reading comprehension. They are innovative in how they accomplish this goal through the use of multiple text sources and multiple answer formats. These materials promote deeper understanding and thought processes by prompting students to analyze, synthesize, hypothesize, and empathize.

✳ **The use of multiple reading sources promotes close reading.**

Close reading is the underlying goal of the Common Core State Standards for English Language Arts. Close reading involves understanding not just the explicit content of a reading passage but also all of the nuances contained therein. A close reading of a text reveals all of the inferential and structural components of the content, while also illuminating the craft that went into the writing of it.

The Common Core State Standards suggest that the best way to foster close reading of informational text is through text complexity. It offers four factors needed to create a high level of text complexity—all four of which are achieved through this book's use of multiple reading sources:

Factor	Meaning
1. Levels of Purpose	The purpose of the text should be implicit, hidden, or obscured in some way.
2. Structure	Texts of high complexity tend to have complex, implicit, or unconventional structures.
3. Language Conventionality or Clarity	Texts should use domain-specific language and feature language that is figurative, ironic, ambiguous, or otherwise unfamiliar.
4. Knowledge Demands	Complex texts make assumptions that readers can use life experiences, cultural awareness, and content knowledge to supplement their understanding of a text.

✳ **The activities prompt students to explore the reading material from all angles.**

By completing the four different activities found in each unit, students will be able to display a broad understanding of the reading material. Each activity and question is designed to make students think about what they have read—everything from how it was written, to why it was written that way, to how its subject matter can be applied to their lives. They gain experience locating information, making inferences from it, and applying knowledge in a variety of ways.

The units in this book are supplemented by a comprehensive answer key (pages 101–108) and a full list of Common Core State Standards correlations (pages 109–112). And even more educational value can be mined from each unit's reading material with "Additional Activities" (page 100). Make copies of this page (one per student per unit) and have students follow the instructions.

How to Use This Book

This book is divided into 28 units, which do not need to be taught in any particular order. Each unit is either three or four pages in length and is composed of reading material (one or two pages) and activity pages (two or three pages):

Reading Material

The reading material for each unit consists of three, four, or five text sources. Have students read all of a unit's text sources before proceeding to the activity pages. These sources complement each other, and a connective thread (or threads) runs throughout them. Sometimes these connections will be explicit, while at other times they will be hidden or obscured.

❋ **Another Approach** After reading the source material, ask students to name all of the ways in which the reading sources seem to be related or connected. See page 100 for more details.

Activity Pages

Each unit is supported by two or three pages of activities. These activity pages are divided into four parts:

Part 1

The Common Core asks students to draw on information from multiple print sources and show the ability to locate an answer to a question quickly or to solve a problem efficiently. This section directly correlates to that standard. Students will gain valuable practice in scanning multiple text sources in order to locate information.

Before beginning this section, remind students to read the directions carefully. Some of the information can be found in two or more sources, which means that students will need to fill in more than one bubble in those instances.

❋ **Another Approach** Have your students practice their recognition of genres and formats. For each unit, have them fill in the chart on page 100.

Part 2

In this section, students are asked to provide the best answer(s) to multiple-choice questions. What sets these apart from the usual multiple-choice questions is their emphasis on higher-order thinking skills. Very few questions ask for simple recall of information. Instead, these questions are designed to provide practice and strengthen knowledge in a variety of areas, including the following:

❋ inference	❋ word etymology	❋ compare and contrast
❋ deduction	❋ parts of speech	❋ cause and effect
❋ grammar and usage	❋ literary devices	❋ analogies
❋ vocabulary in context	❋ authorial intent	❋ computation

❋ **Another Approach** Ask each student to write an original multiple-choice question based on the reading sources. Use the best or most interesting questions to create a student-generated quiz. See page 100 for more details.

How to Use This Book *(cont.)*

Activity Pages *(cont.)*

Part 3

This two-question section takes the skills addressed in Part 1 and approaches them from another angle. Part 3 is in the form of a scavenger hunt that asks students to search the sources in order to locate a word or phrase that fits the criteria described. Students are also asked to name the source in which they found the word or phrase.

> ✳ **Another Approach** Assign students to small groups, and have each group collaboratively come up with two suitable scavenger hunts from the reading material. These student-created scavenger hunts can then be completed and discussed by the entire class. See page 100 for more details.

Part 4

This section is composed of three questions that ask students to integrate information from several texts on the same topic in order to write knowledgeably about a subject. The vast majority of these questions are open-ended, while the rest involve using a new format (e.g., chart, diagram, graph) to organize and/or interpret data and information.

The questions in this section challenge students to blend close-reading concepts with flexible-thinking skills. Students are asked to do the following:

Analyze	Synthesize	Hypothesize	Empathize
✳ authorial choices ✳ intent of characters/ historical figures ✳ overall meanings ✳ quotations in context ✳ statistical data	✳ combine different takes on the same subject ✳ use information from different genres and formats (nonfiction, fiction, graphs, etc.) to draw conclusions ✳ compare and contrast characters, ideas, and concepts ✳ draw conclusions from information and/or numerical data	✳ make predictions about future events ✳ explore alternatives to previous choices	✳ connect to one's own life ✳ put oneself in a character's/ historical figure's place

> ✳ **Another Approach** The Common Core places a strong emphasis on teaching and applying speaking and listening skills. Many of the questions in Part 4 lend themselves well to meeting standards from this strand. Have individual students present oral reports on specific Part 4 questions. Or, form groups of students and ask them to engage in collaborative discussion before presenting their findings.

Kid in a Candy Store

Read each source below. Then complete the activities on pages 7–8.

Source 1

I love games. Give me a puzzle to solve or a high score to aim for, and I'm like a kid in a candy store. I've always been that way.

So when there was a contest at the local mall, you could bet I was going to enter. The contest was to see who could donate the most used-but-in-good-condition clothing. The clothes would then be sold, and the proceeds would go to help those in need.

For two weeks, I was as busy as a bee. I turned all of our closets upside down and inside out. I did the same at the houses of my friends and relatives. Everyone found outfits they had forgotten existed. Great mounds of blouses and enormous piles of pants turned my family garage into a warehouse.

Then the day came. We had to use four cars (Mom's, Dad's, Aunt Bea's, and our neighbor Joe's) to haul the collection to the mall. I knew my donations would outweigh those of the other contestants, and they did. It was no contest.

That's when I found out that Sweet's Sweets had decided to give a prize to the winner. There was a ceremony, and Mr. Sweet presented me with a certificate for a $40 shopping spree at his mall location. I walked into Sweet's Sweets and stared in awe at the shelves overflowing with chocolates and the barrels brimming with butterscotches. Suddenly, I wasn't just *like* a kid in a candy store. I *was* a kid in a candy store. It was the best prize ever!

This certificate good for $40 in free candy at Sweet's Sweets

Source 2

(simile)

a figure of speech that uses a connective word such as *like*, *as*, *so*, or *than* to directly compare two people, things, experiences, etc.

Examples:

* The best friends were like two peas in a pod.

* For the winner, victory tasted as sweet as candy.

Source 3

Sweet's Sweets

"Making Life Sweet Since 1953"

every kind of candy imaginable

$4.25 per pound

Kid in a Candy Store (cont.)

Name: _____

Part 1: Read each idea about Source 1. Which paragraph **introduces** you to this information? Fill in the correct bubble for each paragraph. (Note: More than one bubble may be filled in for each idea.)

Information	Paragraphs ➡	1	2	3	4	5
1. The narrator has an aunt named Bea.		○	○	○	○	○
2. The narrator entered a contest at the mall.		○	○	○	○	○
3. The narrator won the mall contest.		○	○	○	○	○
4. The narrator had help from family and friends.		○	○	○	○	○

Part 2: Fill in the bubble next to the best answer to each question.

5. Which set of words from Source 1 are not used as synonyms in the story?

Ⓐ *mounds* and *piles*   Ⓒ *great* and *enormous*

Ⓑ *haul* and *outweigh*   Ⓓ *overflowing* and *brimming*

6. Estimate to determine about how much candy the narrator of Source 1 can get at Sweet's Sweets with his/her prize.

Ⓐ slightly more than 4 pounds   Ⓒ slightly more than 10 pounds

Ⓑ slightly less than 10 pounds   Ⓓ slightly less than 40 pounds

7. How does the narrator of Source 1 feel when he/she writes in the fourth paragraph, "It was no contest"?

Ⓐ proud   Ⓒ confused

Ⓑ disappointed   Ⓓ as busy as a bee

8. Which word would best describe the narrator of Source 1?

Ⓐ determined   Ⓒ generous

Ⓑ disinterested   Ⓓ inactive

Part 3: Search "Kid in a Candy Store" to find words with the following meanings. (The part of speech is given in parentheses.) Then write the number of the source in which you located this information.

9. "money obtained from an event" (noun) _____   Source #: _____

10. "linking things together" (adjective) _____   Source #: _____

Part 4: Refer back to the sources, and use complete sentences to answer these questions.

11. Literal language describes something as it actually could happen. Figurative language uses colorful comparisons to give a feeling of what is happening. In Source 1, the narrator says, "I turned all of our closets upside down and inside out." Explain why this narrator is using figurative language. In doing so, use literal language to explain what the narrator is actually doing.

_____

_____

_____

_____

12. Picture the area at Sweet's Sweets where you pay for your candy. Which type of measuring equipment would be needed there? Fill in the circle above the correct answer and then explain why this equipment would be needed.

Ⓐ   Ⓑ   Ⓒ   Ⓓ

_____

_____

13. Imagine you have won a shopping spree at your favorite store. Describe what you would buy. Use at least three similes in your paragraph.

_____

_____

_____

_____

_____

_____

_____

The Plutoed Planet

Read each source below. Then complete the activities on pages 10–11.

Source 1

Tri-City Tribune   **May 2, 1930**

Child Names Planet Pluto

The astronomers of Lowell Observatory have voted, and it is official: our solar system's newest planet will be named Pluto. This name was first suggested by Venetia Burney, an 11-year-old schoolgirl from Oxford, England. A fan of mythology, Ms. Burney believed that the planet should be named after Pluto, the Roman god of the cold, dark underworld.

Pluto's journey from discovery to named planet has been quick. It was first observed on February 18 of this year by Clyde Tombaugh at Lowell Observatory in Arizona. On March 24, a vote was held at Lowell Observatory to determine the planet's name. In addition to Pluto, the names Minerva and Cronus were also on the ballot. Yesterday, the results of the vote were announced, and they were unanimous. Every member chose Pluto for the planet's name.

Pluto now joins an exclusive club, as it becomes one of only nine planets in our solar system. Of these, Pluto is the farthest from the Sun. Astronomers believe that it is the coldest and smallest of the nine.

Source 2

Tri-City Tribune   **September 14, 2006**

Pluto Ousted!

Pluto has always been the little planet that was a little different than all the others. Yesterday, the International Astronomical Union (IAU) announced that Pluto will no longer be considered a planet. It will now be classified as a minor planet.

After a vote yesterday, the IAU has officially defined what it means to be a planet in our solar system, and Pluto does not meet all of the criteria. This decision is unpopular with some astronomers, while others believe Pluto should have been stripped of its planet status long ago.

In 1930, Pluto was named the ninth planet in our solar system, despite the fact that it is much smaller than the other eight planets, and its orbit around the Sun follows a different path. With yesterday's ruling, Pluto now becomes just one of the nearly 400,000 minor planets that have been discovered.

Source 3

Tri-City Tribune   **January 6, 2007**

And the Winner Is . . .

2006 was a rough year for the former planet Pluto, but 2007 is starting off much better. Yesterday, the American Dialect Society announced its Word of the Year for 2006, and the honor goes to *plutoed*. This newly created verb means "devalued" or "demoted," and it describes what happened to Pluto when the International Astronomical Union (IAU) decided last year that Pluto no longer met its definition of a planet. By winning this year's award, Pluto finally has something that no one can ever take away.

Name: _____

Part 1: Read each idea. Which source gives you this information? Fill in the correct bubble for each source. (Note: More than one bubble may be filled in for each idea.)

Information	Sources ➡	1	2	3
1. Pluto was named a planet in 1930.		○	○	○
2. Pluto was named a minor planet in 2006.		○	○	○
3. *Plutoed* won Word of the Year in 2006.		○	○	○
4. The IAU voted to change Pluto's planetary status.		○	○	○

Part 2: Fill in the bubble next to the best answer to each question.

5. Earth is a planet. At this time, how many **other** planets are there in our solar system?

 Ⓐ 7   Ⓑ 8   Ⓒ 9   Ⓓ 10

6. If 100 people were asked to vote on the name Pluto, a unanimous vote would mean that

 Ⓐ at least 50 voted in favor of the name.

 Ⓑ more than 50 voted in favor of the name.

 Ⓒ at least 90 voted in favor of the name.

 Ⓓ all 100 voted in favor of the name.

7. Which word best describes the tone of the article in Source 3?

 Ⓐ serious   Ⓒ mean-spirited

 Ⓑ light-hearted   Ⓓ confused

8. Based on how the term is used in Source 1, which of these could be said to belong to an "exclusive club"?

 Ⓐ the stars in the sky

 Ⓑ the number of minor planets in our solar system

 Ⓒ the voting members at Lowell Observatory

 Ⓓ the number of people who have read a newspaper

Part 3: Search "The Plutoed Planet" to find one example of each of the following. Then write the number of the source in which you located this information.

 9. a synonym for "removed" _____ Source #: _____

 10. a synonym for "route" or "trip" _____ Source #: _____

Part 4: Refer back to the sources, and use complete sentences to answer questions #12 and #13.

11. Add the exact dates (month, day, year) in the blank boxes to complete the timeline below.

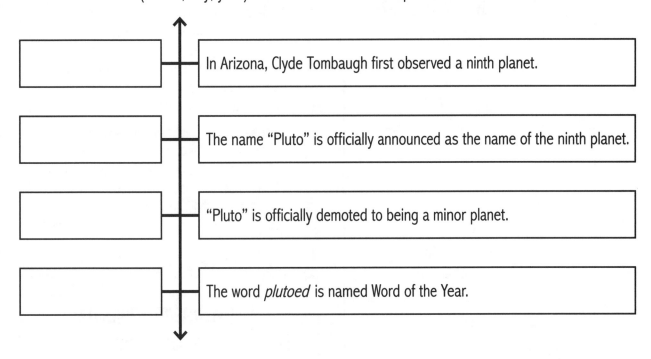

In Arizona, Clyde Tombaugh first observed a ninth planet.

The name "Pluto" is officially announced as the name of the ninth planet.

"Pluto" is officially demoted to being a minor planet.

The word *plutoed* is named Word of the Year.

12. In 1930, when it came time to name the newly discovered planet, why do you think Venetia Burney chose the name Pluto? Why did the astronomers think this was a good choice? Use information from the sources in your answer.

_____

_____

_____

_____

13. Venetia Burney (whose last name became Phair in 1947) lived until 2009. Was she alive when Pluto lost its status as a planet? Imagine being the one who named a planet when you were 11 years old. How would it feel to learn that it would no longer be considered a planet?

_____

_____

_____

_____

_____

Starting at the Source

Read each source below. Then complete the activities on pages 13–15.

Source 1

WELCOME TO MINNESOTA!
"The Land of 10,000 Lakes"

a brochure from the proud citizens of Minnesota

St. Paul○

Admitted to the Union on May 11, 1858

Capital City: St. Paul

Largest City: Minneapolis

Source 2

The following chart lists the 10 states in the U.S. that have the largest area of water. Amounts are given in water area (listed in square miles) and the percentage (%) of the state that is covered in water.

Rank	State	Postal Code	Water Area	% of Area
1	Alaska	AK	94,743	14.24%
2	Michigan	MI	40,175	41.54%
3	Florida	FL	12,133	18.45%
4	Wisconsin	WI	11,339	17.31%
5	Louisiana	LA	9,174	17.52%
6	California	CA	7,916	4.84%
7	New York	NY	7,429	13.62%
8	Texas	TX	7,365	2.74%
9	Minnesota	MN	7,309	8.41%
10	North Carolina	NC	5,201	9.66%

Source 3

In October of 1963, the United States Post Office Department published a list of two-letter abbreviations for all states and territories. Before that, state names were written out in full or written with longer abbreviations (for example, *California* was written as *Calif.*).

These original abbreviations remain in use today, with only one exception: the state of Nebraska initially used the abbreviation "NB." In November of 1969, this was changed to "NE" to avoid confusion with the Canadian province of New Brunswick.

Source 4

WELCOME TO MINNESOTA!
Our State Nickname

When we call ourselves "The Land of 10,000 Lakes," it's not an exaggeration! In fact, Minnesota is home to 11,842 lakes, each at least 10 acres in size. At over 960,000 acres, the Minnesota portion of Lake Superior is the largest and deepest of these lakes. Our state is also home to over 6,500 natural rivers and streams. The place where a river begins is called its **source**, and the place where it ends is called its **mouth**. Lake Itasca in northern Minnesota is the source of the mighty Mississippi River, the largest river in North America. The Mississippi winds southward from Lake Itasca all the way down to Louisiana (LA), where it ends by emptying into the Gulf of Mexico.

page 4

Starting at the Source (cont.)

Name: _____

Part 1: Read each idea. Which source gives you this information? Fill in the correct bubble for each source. (Note: More than one bubble may be filled in for each idea.)

Information	Sources ➡	1	2	3	4
1. State abbreviations haven't changed since 1969.		○	○	○	○
2. Minnesota became a state in 1858.		○	○	○	○
3. Minnesota is nicknamed "The Land of 10,000 Lakes."		○	○	○	○
4. The Mississippi River's source is in Minnesota.		○	○	○	○

Part 2: Fill in the bubble(s) next to the best answer(s) to each question.

5. Which of these lists show the correct order—from greatest to least—of the percentage of the state's area that is covered in water?

Ⓐ Alaska, Michigan, Florida, Wisconsin

Ⓑ Florida, Wisconsin, Alaska, Minnesota

Ⓒ Michigan, Florida, New York, Texas

Ⓓ Florida, Wisconsin, Louisiana, Texas

6. About how many lakes, rivers, and streams does Minnesota have altogether?

Ⓐ just under 12,000　　　　　Ⓒ just over 17,000

Ⓑ just over 16,000　　　　　Ⓓ just over 18,000

7. Which of the following can you infer about the author of Source 4?

Ⓐ He/she was born in Minnesota.　　　　Ⓒ He/she has visited Lake Itasca.

Ⓑ He/she is a citizen of Minnesota.　　　Ⓓ He/she never exaggerates.

8. Which of these underlined words from Source 3 is used as an adverb and means "at first"?

Ⓐ "These <u>original</u> abbreviations"　　　Ⓒ "with only one <u>exception</u>"

Ⓑ "with <u>only</u> one exception"　　　　　Ⓓ "<u>initially</u> used the abbreviation"

Part 3: Search "Starting at the Source" to find one example of each of the following. Then write the number of the source in which you located this information.

9. a common noun with five syllables _____ Source #: _____

10. a proper noun with five syllables _____ Source #: _____

Name: _____

Part 4: Refer back to the sources to answer these questions.

11. How long after the U.S. Post Office published its list of state abbreviations was the abbreviation for Nebraska changed from "NB" to "NE"? Circle **all** correct answers.

| 6 years, 0 months | 6 years, 1 month | 7 years, 0 months | 7 years, 1 month | 61 months | 73 months |

In the space below, use complete sentences to explain how you determined the correct answer(s). Give the data you used, name the source in which you found the data, and explain the math you used.

_____

_____

_____

_____

12. On the blank pages below, create two pages from a brochure about your state.

   ✳ **On the page on the left:** Create the front page of your brochure. Include the name of your state, a drawing of it, and any other basic information.

   ✳ **On the page on the right:** Create an inside page of your brochure. This page can be about anything related to your state. Focus on one aspect of your state—its geography, weather, tourist attractions, sports teams, etc.—it's your choice.

Starting at the Source (cont.)

Name: _____

Part 4 (cont.):

13. Look at the map below of the United States (not including Alaska and Hawaii). Using a black or blue pen and a pencil, do the following:

✱ Use a pen to write in the correct postal abbreviations for Minnesota and Nebraska.

✱ On the lines below the map, write the exact quote from the reading sources that tells you what a river's source and mouth are.

✱ Use a pen to write **"source"** in the state where the Mississippi River begins.

✱ Use a pen to write **"mouth"** in the state where the Mississippi River ends.

✱ Use a pencil to shade in the nine states (not including Alaska) with the largest area(s) of water.

_____

_____

_____

The To-Do List

Read each source below. Then complete the activities on pages 17–18.

Source 1

Official Stationery of
The Byrds

Dear Jay,

Good morning! When I left to take your little sis to preschool, you were sleeping like a baby. You know that saying "the early bird gets the worm"? Well, I guess the late Byrd gets a big to-do list. Sorry, but we need to get a lot done before tomorrow morning's garage sale.

I'm leaving you three $20 bills. Please use them to buy poster supplies at Office World. (Get a few different colors of poster paper.) I wrote the list on a sticky note and put it in the usual place on the fridge. (And if you have time later, you can start making some posters to put around the neighborhood.)

Also, please go to the bank and get some smaller bills and coins. We'll need plenty of change to give people when they buy items at our garage sale. Get lots of ones and fives. Maybe get a ten or two, too. I think one roll of quarters would be a good idea, too. The quarters come in $10 rolls.

As you know, we're mostly going to be selling your sister's old baby clothes and toys. I hope somebody buys the TV, too. That old thing is a dinosaur, but someone might want it. So you can start collecting that stuff and sorting the clothes by sizes. That would be a big help!

Love Mom

Source 2

Little Notes for the Byrds

Poster Supplies Needed

poster paper
markers
glue sticks
wooden stakes

Source 3

Office World
Friday 7/22/16   1:26 p.m.

Item	Quantity	Total
Glue Stick	1 pkg	$1.50
Paper (gray)	4	$2.00
Paper (white)	4	$1.40
Wooden stake	8	$2.00
Markers	1 pkg	$2.00
	Subtotal	$8.90
	Tax	$.78
	Total	**$9.68**
	Paid	$20.00
	Change	$10.32

Unopened items may be returned within 30 days if accompanied by an original receipt.

The To-Do List *(cont.)*

Name: _____

Part 1: Read each idea. Which source gives you this information? Fill in the correct bubble for each source. (Note: More than one bubble may be filled in for each idea.)

Information	Sources ➡	1	2	3
1. Jay's family is having a garage sale.		○	○	○
2. Jay's family needs supplies to make posters.		○	○	○
3. Office World sells supplies for making posters.		○	○	○
4. Office World sells markers and glue sticks.		○	○	○

Part 2: Fill in the bubble next to the best answer to each question.

5. How much does one piece of white poster paper cost at Office World?

   Ⓐ 25¢   Ⓑ 35¢   Ⓒ 40¢   Ⓓ 50¢

6. Near the end of the Source 1 note, Jay's mother writes, "Maybe get a ten or two, too." Which of the following presents a clearer way to say the same thing?

   Ⓐ "Maybe get a $10 bill or a $2 bill, also."

   Ⓑ "Maybe get a $10 bill or two $2 bills, also."

   Ⓒ "Maybe get one or two $10 bills, also."

   Ⓓ "Maybe get a $10 bill or a $20 bill, also."

7. Jay's mother refers to the saying "the early bird gets the worm." What does this saying mean?

   Ⓐ He who wakes up early is rewarded.   Ⓒ He who wakes up late is rewarded.

   Ⓑ He who wakes up early is punished.   Ⓓ He who wakes up early is given a worm.

8. When the mother refers to the TV as a "dinosaur," she is most likely commenting on its _____.

   Ⓐ size and cost   Ⓒ color and appearance

   Ⓑ age and technology   Ⓓ remote control

Part 3: Search "The To-Do List" to find one example of each of the following. Then write the number of the source in which you located this information.

   9. a simile _____ Source #: _____

   10. a possessive noun _____ Source #: _____

Name: _____

Part 4: Refer back to the sources to answer these questions.

11. In Source 1, we learn that a roll of quarters equals $10 dollars.

   A. How many total quarters are there in a $10 roll? _____

   B. In order to answer the previous question of how many quarters equal $10, you need to know a piece of information that is not given in the sources. Use a complete sentence to name that piece of information.

   _____

12.   **A.** After buying supplies from Office World, how much money does Jay have left? (Round your answer to the nearest whole dollar.) _____

   B. How did you find this answer?

   _____

   _____

   C. According to his mother's instructions, Jay needs to use this leftover money to get small bills from the bank. How many of each small bill/coin should he get?

   _____ **$1 bills** _____ **$5 bills** _____ **$10 bills** _1 roll_ **quarters**

   D. Explain why you chose these amounts for problem C.

   _____

   _____

13. Make a poster for the garage sale. On the poster, list the date of the sales, as well as at least two items that will be for sale. Use the information provided in the sources to find this information.

The Botched Batch

Read each source below. Then complete the activities on pages 20–21.

Source 1

Baking Measurements

3 teaspoons = 1 tablespoon

8 tablespoons = $\frac{1}{2}$ cup

16 tablespoons = 1 cup

Source 2

No doubt about it. I got this one. It's in the bag. I will be taking home the blue ribbon this year in my school's annual baking contest. The Thomson sisters—Leah and Grace—won last year's event. I got second place, which was not bad for my first try. But this year, I have a secret weapon. I have Grandma Hannah's Home Run Cookies. Everybody loves them, and they're my ticket to victory.

I've already made the white and red frosting. (White frosting will cover the cookie, while the red frosting will be used to make the stitches on the baseball design.) Now it's time to make some killer cookies! I've decided to double the recipe so everybody can have seconds. Trust me, everybody is going to be talking about these cookies after tomorrow.

In a large mixing bowl, I combine $4\frac{3}{4}$ cups of flour, 1 teaspoon of baking soda, and 1 tablespoon of salt. In a separate bowl, I mix together the rest of the ingredients. Then I mix together the ingredients from both bowls. The result is a fluffy concoction that looks and smells amazing (though I don't taste it because it contains raw eggs, which are not safe to consume).

I roll the dough into balls, coat each ball with sugar, and place them all on baking sheets. Then I pop them into the oven. Soon the sweet smell of victory will waft through my kitchen. This is my year. No doubt about it.

Source 3

RECIPE

Grandma Hannah's Home Run Cookies

Dough Ingredients:

- $2\frac{3}{4}$ cups flour
- 1 teaspoon baking soda
- $\frac{1}{2}$ teaspoon salt
- $1\frac{1}{4}$ cups butter
- 2 cups sugar
- 2 eggs
- 2 teaspoons vanilla extract

Yield: 1 dozen cookies

Source 4

Botched! Bungled! Flubbed! These are the best words to describe my culinary efforts. I was so sure I was going to produce a batch of beautiful baseball cookies, but it was not to be. They looked—and tasted—more like hockey pucks. In hindsight, I probably shouldn't have told my competitors that I was going to bake them all under the table. I dropped the ball on this one, and the real problem is that I have no idea what I did wrong.

Confused and embarrassed,
Andi

The Botched Batch *(cont.)*

Name: _____

Part 1: Read each idea. Which source gives you this information? Fill in the correct bubble for each source. (Note: More than one bubble may be filled in for each idea.)

Information	Sources ➡	1	2	3	4
1. The cookie recipe is from Grandma Hannah.		○	○	○	○
2. Grandma Hannah's recipe requires vanilla extract.		○	○	○	○
3. Grandma Hannah's recipe requires eggs.		○	○	○	○
4. A tablespoon is bigger than a teaspoon.		○	○	○	○

Part 2: Fill in the bubble(s) next to the best answer(s) to each question.

5. From the information, you can infer the narrator of Source 2 is _____.

    Ⓐ Andi   Ⓒ Hannah

    Ⓑ Grace   Ⓓ Leah

6. Which answers show how many cookies the narrator of Source 2 would expect to make after she doubled the recipe?

    Ⓐ 1 dozen   Ⓒ 24

    Ⓑ 2 dozen   Ⓓ 48

7. The first three words of Source 4 are _____ and _____.

    Ⓐ synonyms   Ⓒ words with positive connotations

    Ⓑ antonyms   Ⓓ words with negative connotations

8. Which of these quotes from the sources is **not** an example of figurative langauge?

    Ⓐ "I was going to bake them all under the table"

    Ⓑ "I dropped the ball on this one"

    Ⓒ "The result is a fluffy concoction that looks and smells amazing"

    Ⓓ "the sweet smell of victory will waft through my kitchen"

Part 3: Search "The Botched Batch" to find examples of **adjectives** with each of the following meanings. Then write the number of the source in which you located each adjective.

9. "distinct" or "apart from something else" _____ Source #: _____

10. "having to do with cooking" _____ Source #: _____

Part 4: Refer back to the sources, and use complete sentences to answer these questions.

11. Why did the narrator's cookies not taste or look good? Explain each error the narrator committed when she made the cookies.

_____

_____

_____

_____

_____

12. Language is ironic when it is intended to mean one thing but unexpectedly ends up meaning the opposite thing. Choose a quote from Source 2 and explain why it is ironic considering what happened at the contest.

_____

_____

_____

_____

_____

13. Imagine you are the narrator from Sources 2 and 4, and you are entering the contest the following year. Write down your thoughts on what happened the first two years you participated in the contest and the changes you've made in order to have more success this year. Try to copy the narrator's voice in your writing.

_____

_____

_____

_____

_____

_____

Now Hear This

Read each source below and on page 23. Then complete the activities on pages 24–25.

Source 1

Mr. Boone began, "If I were to ask you what we use to hear all of the sounds there are around us, I bet you would all say 'our ears'. But did you know that there are three main parts to the ear—the inner ear, the middle ear, and the outer ear?"

With this, Mr. Boone projected onto a screen an image of the three parts of the ear.

"Each of these parts serves a vital function. Before we talk about the internal structures that make up the middle ear and inner ear, let's begin where our hearing of sound begins—the outer ear."

Mr. Boone clicked a button, and an image of an outer ear appeared on the screen. "Now, the *pinna*—which is a fancy word for the part of an ear that is visible—has a very distinct shape, doesn't it? We each have two pinnae—one on the left side of the head and one on the right. These pinnae are full of curves and folds. Why do you suppose that is? These curves and folds perform a special function: they help us collect sound and direct it into the ear canal. Once sound enters our ear canal, it goes to the middle ear and then on to the inner ear."

Mr. Boone paused and then continued, "Think of it this way: what do you do if you want to hear something a little bit better?"

The class looked unsure, so Mr. Boone demonstrated as he spoke. "You might cup your hand just behind your ear, right? And why would you do that? By doing that, you create another, even larger fold that helps collect sound and direct it into your ear canal."

Source 2

Three Parts of the Ear

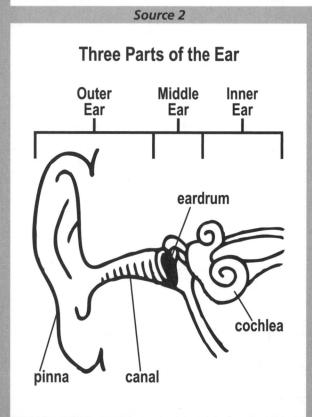

Source 3

The Outer Ear

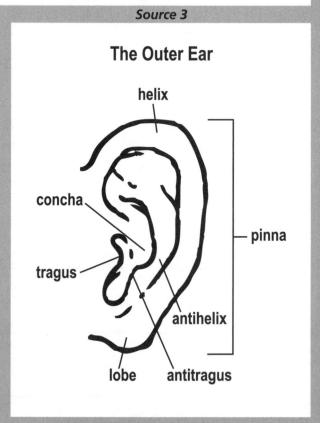

Source 4

January 6, 2017   **Munson Gazette**   *page 5*

YES VOTE BRINGS MUSIC TO MUNSON'S EARS

by Carlton Leftwich

After many false starts and stops, on Thursday the Munson city council finally approved plans to go forward with the building of a new band shell at Hazel Park. The shell will be the centerpiece of the nearly $90,000 renovation scheduled to be completed by early May. The city council hopes to recoup the majority of the costs through a weekly "Saturday in the Park" festival that will feature musical acts, food vendors, and other attractions.

"This plan has been on hold for quite some time," said Munson's mayor, Cindy Banks. "It's a relief to finally get it approved. A weekly festival will be a boon to our local businesses, and it will help establish our town as a destination for visitors coming from far and wide." Mayor Banks went on to say that local musicians and music lovers will be thrilled with the new band shell. "This state-of-the-art structure is going to attract a lot of talented musicians to our beautiful park. And fans of great music will really get to hear each soulful sound the way it's intended to be heard."

Faithful readers of my column know where I stand on this issue: it's long overdue. This is precisely what our tax money should be used for. For years, our city council has been a hindrance. They have prevented progress and refused to inject new ideas into our town. So for those of us who have long been beating the drum of citywide improvement, yesterday's announcement brings music to our ears.

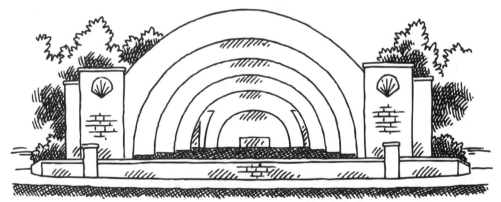

artist's drawing of the proposed band shell at Hazel Park

Name: _____

Part 1: Read each idea. Which source gives you this information? Fill in the correct bubble for each source. (Note: More than one bubble may be filled in for each idea.)

Information	Sources ➡	1	2	3	4
1. There are three main parts to the ear.		◯	◯	◯	◯
2. The outer ear is called the pinna.		◯	◯	◯	◯
3. The eardrum is part of the middle ear.		◯	◯	◯	◯
4. The tragus is part of the outer ear.		◯	◯	◯	◯

Part 2: Fill in the bubble next to the best answer to each question.

5. How is the plural of the word *pinna* formed?

Ⓐ by adding *s*   Ⓒ by adding *e*

Ⓑ by adding *es*   Ⓓ by adding *ae*

6. Which word from Source 4 has a negative connotation?

Ⓐ boon   Ⓒ renovation

Ⓑ hindrance   Ⓓ centerpiece

7. The name of one of the ear's internal structures comes from the Latin word for "snail shell." Based on the diagrams provided, which structure is this?

Ⓐ concha   Ⓒ helix

Ⓑ cochlea   Ⓓ antihelix

8. Picture Mr. Boone as he is speaking in the last paragraph of Source 1. What is he doing?

Ⓐ clicking a button

Ⓑ pointing at his ear

Ⓒ pointing at a diagram of an ear

Ⓓ cupping his hand behind his ear

Part 3: Search "Now Hear This" to find one example of each of the following. Then write the number of the source in which you located this information.

9. a compound word _____ Source #: _____

10. a hyphenated word _____ Source #: _____

Now Hear This (cont.)

Name: _____

Part 4: Refer back to the sources, and use complete sentences to answer these questions.

11. In a newspaper, a column is a regular feature written by a single author, and it usually expresses that author's opinion. Provide two quotes from Source 4 that show it is a column.

_____

_____

_____

_____

12. Look back at Source 3. Choose two of the labeled parts from the diagram. Imagine that you must teach the names of these parts to a friend. Use your own words to describe what each part looks like.

Part	Description

13. Why might a band shell enhance an audience's enjoyment of a musical performance? Use information from at least two sources to provide scientific reasons for your answer.

_____

_____

_____

_____

_____

_____

Coming In with the Comet

Read each source below. Then complete the activities on pages 27–28.

Source 1

Samuel Langhorne Clemens (aka, "Mark Twain")

Born: November 30, 1835

Died: April 21, 1910

Summary: Clemens, writing under the pseudonym Mark Twain, was a very successful American author. He published 13 novels and several short stories. He is known for his great wit and humor. He has been called "the father of American literature," and his *Adventures of Huckleberry Finn* has often been referred to as "the great American novel."

Source 2

-nym
suffix meaning "name"

Examples of words containing **-nym**:

* **eponym** — a discovery, invention, place, etc., named after a person
  * Halley's Comet is named after Edmond Halley, an English astronomer.

* **homonym** — "same name"; includes *homophones* (words that sound the same but have different meanings) and *homographs* (words that are spelled the same but pronounced differently and have different meanings)
  * The words *to*, *too*, and *two* are homophones.
  * The words *lead* (noun) and *lead* (verb) are homographs.

* **pseudonym** — "false name"; a made-up name, often used by artists
  * American author Samuel Longhorne Clemens wrote his books under the pseudonym "Mark Twain."

Source 3

Comets are chunks of ice, dust, and rock that move through space. Some comets make regular passes by Earth. One such comet is called Halley's Comet, and it can be observed from Earth every 75 years or so. The following list shows the years since 1500 in which the comet could be observed from Earth. The exact dates given show when the comet came the closest to the Sun in its orbit.

August 26, 1531
October 27, 1607
September 15, 1682
March 13, 1759
November 16, 1835
April 20, 1910
February 9, 1986
July 28, 2061*

* predicted date

Source 4

"I came in with Halley's Comet in 1835. It is coming again next year, and I expect to go out with it. It will be the greatest disappointment of my life if I don't go out with Halley's Comet."

—*American author Mark Twain, 1909*

Name: _____

Part 1: Read each idea. Which source gives you this information? Fill in the correct bubble for each source. (Note: More than one bubble may be filled in for each idea.)

Information Sources ➡	1	2	3	4
1. Edmond Halley was an English astronomer.	○	○	○	○
2. Mark Twain was an American author.	○	○	○	○
3. "Mark Twain" is a pseudonym.	○	○	○	○
4. Halley's Comet was observed from Earth in 1835.	○	○	○	○

Part 2: Fill in the bubble(s) next to the best answer(s) to each question.

5. How old was Mark Twain when he died?

Ⓐ 65   Ⓑ 75   Ⓒ 74   Ⓓ 64

6. Based on the information given in the sources, what is the meaning of the term *pseudoscience*?

Ⓐ "scientific name"   Ⓒ "science words"

Ⓑ "false science"   Ⓓ "comet science"

7. Which of these words from the sources means "clever intelligence"?

Ⓐ wit   Ⓒ regular

Ⓑ humor   Ⓓ successful

8. Which of the following are **not** homophones?

Ⓐ *rose* (noun) and *rows* (noun)

Ⓑ *rose* (verb) and *rose* (noun)

Ⓒ *rose* (noun) and *flower* (noun)

Ⓓ *flower* (noun) and *flour* (noun)

Part 3: Search "Coming In with the Comet" to find one example of each of the following. Then write the number of the source in which you located this information.

9. a year from the 18th century _____ Source #: _____

10. a title of a novel _____ Source #: _____

Coming In with the Comet *(cont.)*

Name: _____

Part 4: Refer back to the sources, and use complete sentences to answer these questions.

11. Look at the timeline of years Halley's Comet could be observed from Earth. Within each time period, many events happened. For each time period, write one major event from your nation's history that took place between those years.

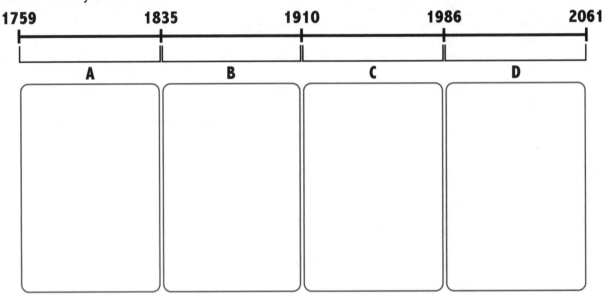

12. What did Mark Twain mean when he said that he "came in" with Halley's Comet and expects to "go out" with it? Did he "go out" with it? Would he have been pleased or disappointed with the timing of these events? Use information from the sources to explain your answers.

_____

_____

_____

_____

_____

13. How old will you be when Halley's Comet can next be observed from Earth? Do you think you will want to see Halley's Comet at that time? Why or why not?

_____

_____

_____

_____

_____

Dawn of a New Day

Read each source below. Then complete the activities on pages 30–31.

Source 1

Hardy's Hardware

owned and operated by
Hal Hardy since 1972

Source 2

Seth Stevens wasn't accustomed to waking up at dawn. The instant his alarm began blaring, Seth's right hand instinctively shot out and smacked the "snooze" button on his clock radio. The room became quiet once more, and Seth resettled his head into his pillow. From somewhere inside his mind, however, a single thought began to peck at his brain. That thought pecked and poked and would not stop. That thought was, "You must get up!" Soon, other thoughts began joining in. "Job!" "Be there by 6 a.m.!" "Hardy's Hardware!" It felt like a barrage of beaks attacking his mind from every angle.

Seth sat up slowly and allowed his eyes to open. It was still dark, with only a hint of light coming in around the edges of his curtains. "Why am I awake right now?" he muttered groggily. That's when the full truth finally dawned on him: today he was beginning his new job at Hardy's Hardware. He had known the owner, Hal Hardy, all his life. He didn't want to disappoint Mr. Hardy by being late on his first day. Reluctantly, Seth stood up and began trudging toward the bathroom. "There will be many Saturday mornings like this one," he thought. "I had better get used to it."

Source 3

I love everything about this time of the day. I love smelling the crisp, cold air and seeing the first traces of the sun as it begins to light the street outside my store. As I open the front door of my shop, the familiar sound of the bell's chime brings a smile to my face. Pride swells inside my chest as I remove the worn gold key from the large silver lock and turn on the overhead lights. I see rows and rows of shelves stocked with tools, ladders, gloves, and everything else anyone would need to make their house a home. The first customer of the day will walk through the door in an hour or so; and in two hours, this place will be a bustling beehive of activity. Saturday mornings are always busy. Right now, however, the store is peaceful and calm. This business has been my life's work since I bought it 37 years ago, and I've loved almost every minute of it.

I whistle a little tune as I begin setting up for the day ahead. I glance at my watch and see that it's 5:55. The Stevens kid should be here any minute. His family has shopped at Hardy's for nearly 20 years, so I practically watched that boy grow up. He's a good kid.

Recently, a new thought has begun to dawn on me: I can't run this hardware store forever. At some point, I'll need to hand over the keys to someone younger. I don't have any children of my own. Who will take care of my store and help it grow? Maybe it will even be Seth Stevens. Who knows? Then again, if he's late on his first day. . . .

Just then I hear the bell chime. "Good morning, boss!"

Dawn of a New Day (cont.)

Name: _____

Part 1: Read each idea. Which source gives you this information? Fill in the correct bubble for each source. (Note: More than one bubble may be filled in for each idea.)

Information	Sources ➡	1	2	3
1. Hardy's Hardware is owned by Hal Hardy		○	○	○
2. Seth Stevens has a job at Hardy's Hardware.		○	○	○
3. Seth's family has shopped at Hardy's Hardware.		○	○	○
4. Seth has known Hal Hardy for a long time.		○	○	○

Part 2: Fill in the bubble(s) next to the best answer(s) to each question.

5. What is the setting of Source 2?

    Ⓐ in a hardware store, at 5:55 a.m.   Ⓒ in a bedroom, at dawn

    Ⓑ in a hardware store, at dawn   Ⓓ in a bedroom, at 5:55 a.m.

6. Which character speaks the final line of Source 3?

    Ⓐ Hal Hardy   Ⓒ the first customer of the day

    Ⓑ Seth Stevens   Ⓓ *none of the above*

7. According to Mr. Hardy, at about what time of day will his store first be very busy?

    Ⓐ at dawn   Ⓒ at 6:00 a.m.

    Ⓑ at noon   Ⓓ at 8:00 a.m.

8. Which two of the following describe how Source 3 is written?

    Ⓐ in present tense   Ⓒ in first person

    Ⓑ in past tense   Ⓓ in third person

Part 3: Search "Dawn of a New Day" to find **adverbs** with the following meanings. Then write the number of the source in which you located each adverb.

    9. "done in a sleepy and unsteady manner" _____   Source #: _____

    10. "done automatically, without thinking" _____   Source #: _____

Dawn of a New Day (cont.)

Name: _____

Part 4: Refer back to the sources, and use complete sentences to answer these questions.

11. On what day of the week and in what year do Sources 2 and 3 take place?

Day of the Week: _____ Year: _____

Explain the information you used to determine your answers.

_____

_____

_____

_____

12. In writing, personification is the use of a person, animal, or object to represent a quality, concept, or thing. Give an example of personification from one of the sources. Explain what the author is attempting to show by using personification in this way.

_____

_____

_____

_____

_____

13. The title of this unit is "Dawn of a New Day." Explain how this title relates to both of the main characters in this unit.

_____

_____

_____

_____

_____

_____

_____

_____

_____

Drawing Conclusions

Read each source below. Then complete the activities on pages 33–35.

Source 1

Mr. Kline said, "Everyone get out a piece of paper and a pencil. We're going to try an exercise in giving and following directions."

There was a brief commotion as all 30 students rummaged through their bags and desks to find the necessary supplies.

"Alright," continued Mr. Kline, "I am going to show you a picture. On your papers, I would like each of you to write a set of directions that explain how to draw the picture. You can do this any way you want to. Your main goal is to make your directions very clear and very easy to follow. You must do this without saying what the final picture will look like. Anyone who uses your directions should be able to draw each part of the picture without knowing what the end result will be. Any questions? Okay, here is the picture."

And with that, Mr. Kline projected this image onto the white screen in front of the class:

Source 2

Drawing Directions

by Freddy Collins

Start by drawing a big square, and then put a little circle in the middle of it. Color it in. Above that circle, draw two smaller circles. They should be to the left and the right. Color them in.

Then draw a small heart below the bigger circle. After that, draw lines coming out of each side of the big circle. Make those lines long. Finally, draw a tall oval on each side of the square, and color those ovals brown.

Source 3

Steps for Drawing

by Ellie Fox

1. In the center of your paper, draw a square the size of your fist.

2. In the center of the square, draw a circle the size of your thumbnail. Shade in the circle with your pencil.

3. Underneath the circle—but not touching it—draw a heart that is about the same size as the circle.

4. Halfway between the circle and the top of the square, draw two circles the same size as the heart you just drew. One circle should be to the left of the center, and the other should be to the right. There should be about an inch of space between the two circles. Darken in these two circles.

5. On each side of the center circle, draw three lines. All of the lines should start at the circle and be drawn outward. The lines should be long enough to go just outside the edge of the square. There will be a total of six lines, three on each side.

6. On each side of the square, draw an oval. Both ovals should be as tall as the square, but not very wide. Each oval should touch the square. Color the ovals brown.

Source 4

Animal Face

by Jenny Evers

This is super easy, Mr. Kline! Just draw a big square in the middle of your paper. That will be the animal's face. In the center of the circle, draw a dark circle to be its nose. Add whiskers on both sides of the nose. Above the nose, add two dark circles for eyes. Draw a little heart for the animal's mouth, and add ears on the sides of its head. The ears should be brown ovals.

Name: _____

Part 1: Read each idea. Which source gives you this information? Fill in the correct bubble for each source. (Note: More than one bubble may be filled in for each idea.)

Information	Sources ➡	1	2	3	4
1. There are 30 students in Mr. Kline's class.		○	○	○	○
2. Jenny Evers is a student in Mr. Kline's class.		○	○	○	○
3. The drawing the class is describing is of an animal's face.		○	○	○	○
4. The drawing includes six lines for whiskers.		○	○	○	○

Part 2: Fill in the bubble(s) next to the best answer(s) to each question.

5. Which student forgets to give a direction for drawing the whiskers?

Ⓐ Freddy   Ⓒ Jenny

Ⓑ Ellie   Ⓓ They all remember.

6. Mr. Kline says, "Anyone who uses your directions should be able to draw each part of the picture without knowing what the end result will be." Which student fails to follow this direction?

Ⓐ Freddy   Ⓒ Jenny

Ⓑ Ellie   Ⓓ All follow this direction.

7. Which shapes are **not** used in the drawing of the animal's face?

Ⓐ ovals   Ⓒ rectangles

Ⓑ circles   Ⓓ triangles

8. We get to see the directions created by three of the students in the class. Which of these numbers does **not** represent the portion of the class whose work we get to see?

Ⓐ $\frac{3}{30}$ Ⓑ $\frac{1}{10}$ Ⓒ $\frac{3}{10}$ Ⓓ 10%

Part 3: Search "Drawing Conclusions" to find one example of each of the following. Then write the number of the source in which you located this information.

9. a synonym for "searched" _____ Source #: _____

10. a word meaning "noisy disturbance" _____ Source #: _____

Drawing Conclusions *(cont.)*

Name: _____

Part 4: Refer back to the sources, and use complete sentences to answer these questions.

11. In your opinion, which student's directions are the clearest and easiest to follow? Give at least three reasons why this student's directions would be the most helpful to someone trying to draw the picture.

_____

_____

_____

_____

_____

_____

_____

12. When giving instructions, it is often helpful to include temporal words. These are words such as *first*, *next*, *then*, and *lastly*. Temporal words make the order of instructions very clear.

Which student used temporal words often in his/her instructions? _____

Write a short paragraph in which you describe why temporal words might make directions easier to follow. In your paragraph, use at least three temporal words.

_____

_____

_____

_____

_____

_____

_____

_____

Drawing Conclusions *(cont.)*

Name: _____

Part 4 *(cont.)*:

13. Look at the drawing below. Write a set of directions that someone could use to create this drawing. Make your directions clear and easy to follow. Do not mention what object the drawing will look like when it is completed.

_____

_____

_____

_____

_____

_____

_____

_____

_____

_____

_____

_____

_____

_____

_____

_____

_____

_____

A Silent Start

Read each source below. Then complete the activities on pages 37–38.

The Great Lakes are five connected lakes located on the continent of North America. They form the largest group of freshwater lakes on Earth. Together, they contain just over 20% of the world's surface fresh water.

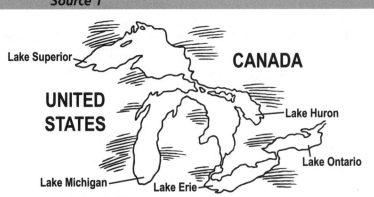

Lake Superior

CANADA

UNITED STATES

Lake Huron

Lake Ontario

Lake Michigan

Lake Erie

Miss Pell wrote "ROY G. BIV" on the board at the front of the class. She said, "Roy G. Biv sounds like a person, but it is not. Roy is a *m-n-e-m-o-n-i-c*. This word is pronounced *ni-mon-ik*. The beginning *m* is completely silent. *Mnemonics* like Roy can help you remember answers. They are memory tricks. When you think of the word *mnemonic*, think of the word *memory*. Both words have two *m*s in them."

Miss Pell continued, "Think about rainbows. We see the seven colors of the rainbow in a specific order. Roy G. Biv tells us the exact order of the colors of the rainbow: red, orange, yellow, green, blue, indigo, and violet. Notice the first letter of each of those color words. When you put those first letters in order, it spells 'Roy G. Biv.' Another mnemonic is 'My Very Educated Mother Just Served Us Nachos.' People use this one to remember the order of the planets from the Sun in our solar system. The first letter of each word in that mnemonic begins with the first letter of the name of a planet. 'My' is for Mercury, 'Very' is for Venus, and so on. Any quick saying or word that jogs your memory and helps you recall information can be a mnemonic. Even *my* name can be mnemonic. People often misspell the word *misspell*, but you never have to again. Just think of my name, and you will always have the perfect way to remember how to spell this word."

Honestly, the hour after lunch is my favorite part of the day. That's when Miss Pell teaches us new words and inspires us to use our imaginations. She even has a group of us creating a class novel. It's a thriller that begins with the sound of a *tap tap tap* on a door. The hero inside the house wakes up and goes to answer the door, but there's no one there. Was she wrong? Did no one knock? Then she hears it again—but louder this time—and she realizes that the sound is coming from a door she never knew was there!

That's how the first chapter ends. From there, each of the 12 students in our group will get to write one chapter, and it will take the whole year to complete. Nobody knows what the final book will be like. Secretly, I'm hoping I get to do that 13th chapter. What an honor that would be!

At the end, the class will decide on a title for the book, and we will also choose a *pseudonym* to call ourselves. Miss Pell taught us that word. It means 'false name', and it is pronounced *soo-doh-nim*. I wonder what we'll come up with. Miss Pell suggested using the first letters of each of our names and rearranging them to make a new name. Maybe we'll do that.

A Silent Start *(cont.)*

Name: _____

Part 1: Read each idea. Which source gives you this information? Fill in the correct bubble for each source. (Note: More than one bubble may be filled in for each idea.)

Information	Sources ➡	1	2	3
1. Miss Pell is a teacher.		○	○	○
2. Miss Pell's name can be a mnemonic.		○	○	○
3. The word *pseudonym* means "false name."		○	○	○
4. Lake Erie is bordered by Canada to the north.		○	○	○

Part 2: Fill in the bubble next to the best answer to each question.

5. How much of the world's surface fresh water is **not** located in the Great Lakes?

Ⓐ just under 20%

Ⓑ just over 20%

Ⓒ just under 80%

Ⓓ just over 80%

6. Which of these things is **not** true about the way the words *pseudonym* and *mnemonic* are pronounced?

Ⓐ Both have three syllables.

Ⓑ Both begin with silent letters.

Ⓒ Both contain a silent *m*.

Ⓓ Both contain the *n* sound.

7. A crayon company is creating new colors. One color combines the name of the 8th planet from the Sun with the name of the 5th color of the rainbow (starting from red). What is the name of this color?

Ⓐ Saturn Indigo

Ⓑ Neptune Blue

Ⓒ Jupiter Green

Ⓓ Uranus Violet

8. Source 3 contains many words that begin with a completely silent letter. How many? After filling in the bubble next to your answer, write each word on the lines below.

Ⓐ 7　　　　　　Ⓑ 8　　　　　　Ⓒ 9　　　　　　Ⓓ 10

_____

_____

Part 3: Search "A Silent Start" to find words with each of the following meanings. Then write the number of the source in which you located this information.

9. "putting in a different order" _____ Source #: _____

10. "to spell incorrectly" _____ Source #: _____

Name: _____

Part 4: Refer back to the sources to answer these questions.

11. In Source 2, Miss Pell provides a mnemonic for remembering how to spell the word *mnemonic*. Find the two-sentence quote from Miss Pell, and write it in the box below.

12. One way that many people remember the names of the Great Lakes is by using a mnemonic. They use the first letter of each lake's name to create a word. What real word can you create by doing this? Write it in the box, and then tell if you think this would help you remember the names of the Great Lakes. Why or why not?

_____

_____

_____

_____

_____

13. In the space below, write the first few paragraphs of the second chapter of the book described in Source 3. Answer such questions as . . .

✳ What is the hero's name?   ✳ Who (or what) is behind the door?

_____

_____

_____

_____

_____

_____

_____

_____

_____

_____

What Is Irrelevant?

Read each source below. Then complete the activities on pages 40–41.

Source 1

| relevant
adjective | significant, important to the matter at hand
antonyms: insignificant, irrelevant |

Source 2

There are several prefixes that can be added to a word in place of the word ***not***. They are called negative prefixes, and they change a word to mean its opposite.

Prefix	Root Words Beginning With	Examples		
dis-	a vowel or consonant	agree → disagree	comfort → discomfort
il-	the letter *l*	legal → illegal	logical → illogical
im-	the letters *m* or *p*	mature → immature	possible → impossible
in-	a vowel (*a*, *e*, or *o*) or a consonant	accurate → inaccurate	correct → incorrect
ir-	the letter *r*	regular → irregular	relevant → irrelevant
un-	a vowel or consonant	clear → unclear	usual → unusual

Source 3

THE GREENDALE GAZETTE

May 24, 2037   "Greendale's News Source Since 1912"

LOCAL PLAYER AIMS TO BE RELEVANT

It was a long wait for Greendale's own Drew Ames, but he finally heard his name. Saturday was the final day of the National Football League's yearly draft of college players. For three days each May, teams from the National Football League (NFL) select college players to be a part of their teams. Someone has to be chosen first, and someone has to be chosen last. At around 3:00 p.m. local time on Saturday—exactly 51 hours after the Minnesota Vikings took quarterback Joe Kennedy with the 1st pick—the Denver Broncos selected Drew Ames with the 256th and final choice of the 2037 draft.

Ames, a wide receiver from Monmouth University, still holds several scoring and receiving records at Greendale High School. "Because I went to a smaller college, I didn't think I'd even be drafted," said Ames. "I'm ready to show the Broncos that they made the right choice." As the final pick, Ames faces a tough uphill battle to make the team. Broncos coach A.J. Hughes said, "He'll have to earn a spot on our team, but we think he can do it. We wouldn't have chosen him if we didn't think he was a good player."

By being the draft's final pick, Ames earned more than just a chance to be a professional football player: he also earned the title "Mr. Irrelevant." Since 1976, the final player taken in each NFL draft has been crowned Mr. Irrelevant and awarded a trip to Newport Beach, California, where a ceremony is held in his honor. While some view this prize as an insult, others interpret the word "irrelevant" a little differently. Does it mean that the last player chosen is irrelevant, and he won't matter to the team? Or does it mean that where he was chosen in the draft is irrelevant, and it's now in his power to show that he belongs? This fall, Drew Ames and the Broncos will look to answer these questions.

What Is Irrelevant? *(cont.)*

Name: _____

Part 1: Read each idea. Which source gives you this information? Fill in the correct bubble for each source. (Note: More than one bubble may be filled in for each idea.)

Information Sources ➡	1	2	3
1. *Dis-* and *un-* are negative prefixes.	○	○	○
2. The last pick of the NFL draft wins a prize.	○	○	○
3. The word *irrelevant* is the opposite of *relevant*.	○	○	○
4. The first Mr. Irrelevant was named in 1976.	○	○	○

Part 2: Fill in the bubble(s) next to the best answer(s) to each question.

5. Which of these words from Source 3 are synonyms for *picked*?

    Ⓐ drafted   Ⓒ earned

    Ⓑ crowned   Ⓓ chosen

6. Which compound word from Source 3 tells you that it will be difficult for Drew Ames to make the football team?

    Ⓐ irrelevant   Ⓒ uphill

    Ⓑ tough   Ⓓ insult

7. Look at the last sentence of the second paragraph in the newspaper article in Source 3. To whom does the pronoun *we* refer?

    Ⓐ the National Football League

    Ⓑ the Denver Broncos

    Ⓒ the people of Greendale

    Ⓓ all of the drafted players

8. In Source 3, we learn that Joe Kennedy was picked first and Drew Ames was picked last. How many other players were picked in the 2037 NFL draft?

    Ⓐ 253   Ⓑ 254   Ⓒ 255   Ⓓ 256

Part 3: Search "What Is Irrelevant?" to find one example of the following. Then write the number of the source in which you located this information.

    9. a word with five syllables _____ Source #: _____

    10. a possessive noun _____ Source #: _____

What Is Irrelevant? *(cont.)*

Name: _____

Part 4: Refer back to the sources, and use complete sentences to answer these questions.

11. At what time and on what day was Joe Kennedy chosen by the Minnesota Vikings? Circle your choice, and then explain how you came up with this answer.

12:00 p.m.	**12:00 p.m.**	**3:00 p.m.**	**3:00 p.m.**
Thursday	**Friday**	**Thursday**	**Saturday**

_____

_____

_____

12. Look again at the headline for the article in Source 3. The writer used the verb *aims*, but several other words with the same meaning could have been used instead. Think of three other words that could have been used.

_____   _____   _____

Now explain why one of your words would have been better or why the word *aims* was the perfect choice for this headline.

_____

_____

_____

13. What do you think is the meaning of the title Mr. Irrelevant? Should someone be proud or insulted to be called that? How would you feel about it if you were picked last and given that title? Explain your answers.

_____

_____

_____

_____

_____

_____

_____

_____

The Chosen Four

Read each source below. Then complete the activities on pages 43–45.

Source 1

Mount Rushmore

the presidents on Mount Rushmore (from left to right): George Washington, Thomas Jefferson, Theodore Roosevelt, Abraham Lincoln

▲ monument carved into the Black Hills in South Dakota, U.S.A.

▲ features 60-foot sculptures of the heads of four U.S. presidents: George Washington (1789–1797), Thomas Jefferson (1801–1809), Abraham Lincoln (1861–1865), Theodore Roosevelt (1901–1909)

▲ construction led by Danish-American sculptor Gutzon Borglum (who chose the four presidents to be depicted) and his son, Lincoln Borglum (who was named after Abraham Lincoln)

▲ construction began on October 4, 1927

▲ construction completed on October 31, 1941

▲ attracts over 2 million visitors per year

Source 2

> **"on the Mount Rushmore of . . ."**
>
> *idiom*

Meaning: The four things, people, places, etc., that could be considered the greatest of any given subject.

Example: Henry says that a cat, a dog, a fish, and a bird would be on the Mount Rushmore of the world's greatest pets.

Source 3

Dear Diary,

So tired. Long plane flight back from South Dakota. Visited Mount Rushmore while I was there. An absolute thrill very awe-inspiring and such enormous heads! How did they carve those heads into the face of that mountain? Whoever picked those presidents, chose wisely. Each so important to our nation's history.

I think Mount Rushmore is on my Mount Rushmore of greatest places I've visited. (Hahaha) Right up there with the Grand Canyon, the Golden Gate Bridge, and the Statue of Liberty. Hmm, what do those four have in common? Gigantic and symbols of America, I suppose.

That's all for now it's time for some shuteye.

Tess

The Chosen Four (cont.)

Name: _____

Part 1: Read each idea. Which source gives you this information? Fill in the correct bubble for each source. (Note: More than one bubble may be filled in for each idea.)

Information	Sources ➡	1	2	3
1. Mount Rushmore is located in South Dakota.		○	○	○
2. Mount Rushmore is a major tourist attraction.		○	○	○
3. Mount Rushmore depicts four presidents.		○	○	○
4. The Statue of Liberty is a symbol of America.		○	○	○

Part 2: Fill in the bubble(s) next to the best answer(s) to each question.

5. If the faces on Mount Rushmore were to go in chronological order from left to right, which two presidents would need to switch places?

Ⓐ Roosevelt and Lincoln   Ⓒ Jefferson and Roosevelt

Ⓑ Jefferson and Lincoln   Ⓓ Washington and Jefferson

6. In which of the following ways is Abraham Lincoln different from the other presidents on Mount Rushmore?

Ⓐ He served during the 19th century.

Ⓑ He served fewer than 8 years.

Ⓒ His term began during an odd-numbered year.

Ⓓ He comes first when listed in alphabetical order by last name.

7. Which part of speech is the underlined word in the following sentence from Source 3?

"Whoever picked those presidents, chose <u>wisely</u>."

Ⓐ noun   Ⓑ verb   Ⓒ adjective   Ⓓ adverb

8. You can infer that Gutzon Borglum admired Abraham Lincoln because

Ⓐ he chose Lincoln to be one of the presidents on Mount Rushmore.

Ⓑ he took the most care when sculpting Lincoln's head.

Ⓒ he voted for Abraham Lincoln twice.

Ⓓ he named his son after Abraham Lincoln.

Part 3: Search "The Chosen Four" to find one example of each of the following. Then write the number of the source in which you located this information.

9. a slang word for "sleep" _____ Source #: _____

10. a possessive noun _____ Source #: _____

The Chosen Four *(cont.)*

Name: _____

Part 4: Refer back to the sources, and use complete sentences to answer these questions.

11. The diary entry in Source 3 contains many sentence fragments and run-on sentences. Edit and rewrite the entry on the lines below. Make sure all sentences are complete.

_____

_____

_____

_____

_____

_____

_____

_____

12. Look at the blank timeline below. The final entry is filled in. Write in the year for this final entry. Then add four events that were mentioned in the sources. These events must be in chronological order, from oldest to most recent.

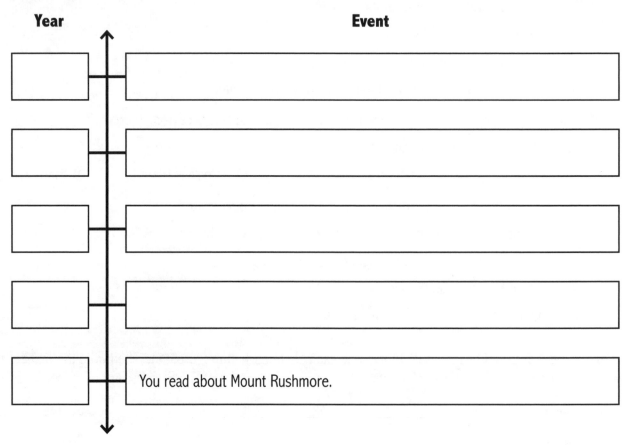

Year	Event
	You read about Mount Rushmore.

Unit 12

The Chosen Four *(cont.)*

Name: ____

13. It's time for you to name your Mount Rushmore of a particular subject. Choose one of the following and circle it. Then, on the lines below, name the four greatest of that subject, and explain why each belongs on your Mount Rushmore. In the box at the bottom, draw a picture of your very own Mount Rushmore.

actors	**athletes**	**singers**
foods	**hobbies**	**video games**

The Mount Rushmore of ______________________________

Even the Odd Ones

Read each source below. Then complete the activities on pages 47–48.

Source 1

even

adjective
1. any number that is divisible by two
2. having a flat, smooth, level surface
3. calm, balanced
4. as likely as not (example, an *even* chance)

adverb
1. used to stress something that is surprising or unlikely
2. used to stress the difference between things that are being compared

Source 2

odd

adjective
1. a number that leaves a remainder of one when divided by two
2. different from what is ordinary or expected

noun (odds)
1. the probability that something will happen
2. in disagreement (with the word *at*)

Source 3

Rick and I had just bought some ice cream from Friend's Frozen Treats. I bought a cone with cherry chocolate chip, and Rick purchased a cup with white chocolate macadamia. We were relaxing and eating ice cream and talking about sports. Then Audrey walked by.

Audrey's my neighbor, and she can seem a bit peculiar. She's very smart and knows a lot of stuff. It's just that sometimes she doesn't even say "hello" before she starts sharing odd information.

She often walks by Friend's on the way to the library, so the odds were good that I'd see her that day. I waved and said, "Hello, Audrey. Are you headed to the library today?"

"You know," she said, "eating ice cream on the sidewalk is illegal in at least one U.S. city."

Rick nearly spit out a nut. "What? That can't be true!"

I smiled a little to myself. I knew better than to question one of my neighbor's claims.

"It's very true," asserted Audrey. "In one city, it's also against the law to eat ice cream in public with a fork. And in another city, you can't keep an ice-cream cone in your back pocket. A police officer could give you a ticket for that."

Rick was shaking his head and getting ready to challenge Audrey. I didn't want to see my friend and my neighbor at odds, so I spoke up, "I had no idea there were so many weird rules about ice cream."

Audrey nodded. "There are a lot of bizarre laws like that. They may sound outlandish or unusual, but you had better not break them. Even a silly law could end up costing you money. Or worse, you could get thrown in jail. Okay, I'm in a hurry." And with that, Audrey scampered off, leaving Rick and I standing there eating our ice cream.

Even the Odd Ones (cont.)

Name: _____

Part 1: Read each idea. Which source gives you this information? Fill in the correct bubble for each source. (Note: More than one bubble may be filled in for each idea.)

Information	Sources ➡	1	2	3
1. The word *even* can be used as an adjective.		○	○	○
2. The word *odd* can be used as an adjective.		○	○	○
3. You are at odds with someone you disagree with.		○	○	○
4. Having "good odds" means a thing is likely to happen.		○	○	○

Part 2: Fill in the bubble next to the best answer to each question.

5. The narrator of Source 3 thinks that being around Audrey isn't very _____.

   Ⓐ odd   Ⓒ relaxing

   Ⓑ even   Ⓓ interesting

6. Which of these words from Source 3 is **not** a synonym for *odd*?

   Ⓐ peculiar   Ⓒ outlandish

   Ⓑ bizarre   Ⓓ illegal

7. Which word from the sources can be a synonym for *emphasis*?

   Ⓐ chance   Ⓒ stress

   Ⓑ probability   Ⓓ divisible

8. The title of this unit ("Even the Odd Ones") most likely refers to _____.

   Ⓐ laws   Ⓒ words

   Ⓑ cities   Ⓓ ice-cream flavors

Part 3: Search "Even the Odd Ones" to find one example of each of the following. Then write the number of the source in which you located this information.

9. a specific type of nut _____ Source #: _____

10. a type of eating utensil _____ Source #: _____

Part 4: Refer back to the sources, and use complete sentences to answer these questions.

11. Of the following words used in the sources, which one is used as a possessive proper noun? Circle your answer and explain why it is a possessive proper noun. Then explain why the other two choices are not.

"<u>Audrey's</u> my neighbor"	"She often walks by <u>Friend's</u>"	"my <u>neighbor's</u> claims"

_____

_____

_____

_____

_____

12. Does the narrator of Source 3 believe Audrey when she talks about strange ice-cream laws? In your answer, use a quote from the source as evidence to back up your claim.

_____

_____

_____

_____

_____

13. The author of Source 3 tries to portray Audrey as being a bit odd. Which character in Source 3 does the author seem to portray as the most even? Give evidence for your answer.

_____

_____

_____

_____

_____

Learning the Lingo

Read each source below. Then complete the activities on pages 50–51.

Source 1

contranym

a word that can mean the opposite of itself; also called a **Janus word** (after the Roman god Janus)

Example: **clip**

1. (*cut away*) I <u>clip</u> coupons out of the newspaper every Sunday.

2. (*attach*) I <u>clip</u> the coupons to my grocery list so I don't lose them.

Source 2

acronym

a word formed from the beginning letters of other words

Examples:

- <u>scuba</u> (<u>s</u>elf-<u>c</u>ontained <u>u</u>nderwater <u>b</u>reathing <u>a</u>pparatus)

- ZIP code (<u>Z</u>one <u>I</u>mprovement <u>P</u>lan)

Source 3

lingo

the special language used by a particular group of people

synonyms and other related words:

- argot
- slang
- jargon
- vernacular

Source 4

Janice couldn't understand why her grandson always referred to his favorite baseball player as a goat. She and Phil watched many games together during the summer, and whenever his favorite player blasted a mammoth home run or made a spectacular leaping catch, Phil would exclaim, "That's why he's the goat!"

Why would a great player be called a goat? Janice couldn't think of a single thing a goat did that was like hitting or fielding a baseball. She asked, "Am I missing something? Why do you keep calling him 'the goat'?"

"Because that's what he is," said Phil.

That was not helpful, she thought.

So, she asked her husband, Lou, how a baseball player could be like a goat. He immediately answered, "They call 'em goats when they make a mistake so dumb that it makes their team lose. No athlete wants to wear the goat's horns."

Now she was really puzzled. Phil was clearly not saying that his favorite player was doing something wrong.

Finally, she approached her son Paul and asked him. She mentioned what Lou said, too.

Phil's dad laughed, "They're both right! When I was growing up, 'goat' was a terrible title to earn in sports. It meant that you made an infamous error that cost your team the game. But now, sports fans use 'G.O.A.T.' differently. The letters 'G.O.A.T.' stand for 'Greatest of All Time.'"

Janice chuckled. "That explains it! I guess I need to learn the lingo of this younger generation of sports fans. Some words mean the opposite of what they used to!"

Learning the Lingo *(cont.)*

Name: _____

Part 1: Read each idea. Which source gives you this information? Fill in the correct bubble for each source. (Note: More than one bubble may be filled in for each idea.)

Information	Sources ➡	1	2	3	4
1. *Slang* is a synonym for *lingo*.		○	○	○	○
2. Sports fans often share a lingo.		○	○	○	○
3. Contranyms are also called Janus words.		○	○	○	○
4. Some words can mean the opposite of themselves.		○	○	○	○

Part 2: Fill in the bubble next to the best answer to each question.

5. Which character in Source 4 seems to best understand the lingo of more than one generation of sports fans?

    Ⓐ Janice   Ⓑ Paul   Ⓒ Phil   Ⓓ Lou

6. Which word from Source 4 could be defined as "well known for some bad deed"?

    Ⓐ mistake   Ⓒ infamous

    Ⓑ mammoth   Ⓓ referred

7. In the meaning of the acronym *scuba*, which word functions as the noun?

    Ⓐ self-contained   Ⓒ breathing

    Ⓑ underwater   Ⓓ apparatus

8. A family tree is a diagram used to show the generations of a family. The eldest generation is usually at the top. Which of these family trees correctly shows the relationship of the characters in Source 4?

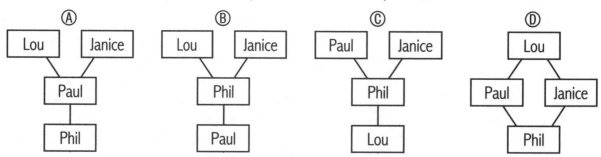

Part 3: Search "Learning the Lingo" to find **four-syllable words** with each of the following meanings. Then write the number of the source in which you located this information.

9. "truly amazing" _____ Source #: _____

10. "a stage in the development of something" _____ Source #: _____

Part 4: Refer back to the sources, and use complete sentences to answer these questions.

11. The following two sentences each contain a contranym. Choose one and name the contranym in the sentence. Explain how it is used in two opposite ways.

    A. The alarm went off and woke us all up, until Ted finally turned it off.

    B. When we left the stadium, there were still 20 minutes left in the game.

_____

_____

_____

_____

_____

12. In Source 4, the term "G.O.A.T." functions in many ways. It is an acronym, it is one half of a contranym, and it is an example of lingo. In paragraph form, explain how this one term functions in each of these ways in Source 4.

_____

_____

_____

_____

_____

_____

_____

_____

13. You probably share a lingo with your friends or your family (or both). What are the benefits of sharing a special language with a group of people? Explain your answer.

_____

_____

_____

_____

_____

Reaching New Heights

Read each source below and on page 53. Complete the activities on pages 54–55.

Source 1

The World's Tallest Buildings
(from 1913 to present)

Year	Building	Location	Height (in Feet)	Number of Floors Above Ground
1913	Woolworth Building	New York City, New York, U.S.A.	792	57
1930	Bank of Manhattan Trust Building	New York City, New York, U.S.A.	927	71
1930	Chrysler Building	New York City, New York, U.S.A.	1,046	77
1931	Empire State Building	New York City, New York, U.S.A.	1,250	102
1972	World Trade Center	New York City, New York, U.S.A.	1,368	110
1974	Sears Tower	Chicago, Illinois, U.S.A.	1,451	108
1998	Petronas Towers	Kuala Lumpur, Malaysia	1,483	88
2004	Taipei 101	Taipei, Taiwan	1,671	101
2010	Burj Khalifa	Dubai, United Arab Emirates	2,717	163

Source 2

"to reach new heights"

idiom

Meaning: "to achieve more success or improvement than ever before."

Source 3

chronological

adjective

in time order, starting with the earliest

from the Greek word *khronos* meaning "time"

Source 4

Australian Climber Reaches New Heights

by Maisy O'Day

New York, NY, February 5, 2014: Pulling weeds? Reading a dictionary from cover to cover? Going to the dentist? These are things that sound a little more fun to me than running up 86 flights of stairs. However, each and every year, that is just what hundreds of athletes line up to do. It's called the Empire State Building Run-Up, and it's been happening inside this New York City skyscraper every year since 1978. One Australian athlete in particular has shown that she is very good at this specialty race. Her name is Suzy Walsham, and she was the fastest female climber for the fifth time. That is a record.

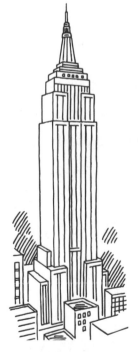

In order to win this race, an athlete has to be the fastest to race up 1,576 steps to the observation deck on the Empire State Building's 86th floor. Suzy held the honor in 2007, 2008, and 2009. It was not until 2013, however, that she was able to win her 4th race, tying the record for most races won by a woman. This year, she raced up the stairs in just under 12 minutes to win her record-setting title. A German athlete named Thomas Dold won seven consecutive times (2006–2012) to hold the overall record.

So, does reading this inspire you to start training for next year's race? Will you be the next great athlete to reach new heights? I think I'd rather go to the dentist or pull weeds, instead.

Empire State Building

Name: _____

Part 1: Read each idea. Which source gives you this information? Fill in the correct bubble for each source. (Note: More than one bubble may be filled in for each idea.)

Information	Sources ➡	1	2	3	4
1. The Empire State Building is in New York City.		○	○	○	○
2. The Empire State Building has over 80 floors.		○	○	○	○
3. The Empire State Building has exactly 102 floors.		○	○	○	○
4. In 2000, the world's tallest building was in Malaysia.		○	○	○	○

Part 2: Fill in the bubble(s) next to the best answer(s) to each question.

5. Which of these statements about the Empire State Building are still true?

Ⓐ It is a skyscraper.

Ⓑ It is the world's tallest building.

Ⓒ It is the tallest building in the U.S.A.

Ⓓ It is the site each year of a race.

6. How many years after the Empire State Building was built was the Run-Up first run?

Ⓐ 47   Ⓑ 57   Ⓒ 58   Ⓓ 63

7. Which statement is the most true about Maisy O'Day's article?

Ⓐ She only reports the facts about the story.

Ⓑ She will probably train to compete in the next Run-Up.

Ⓒ She often states her opinions about the events in her article.

Ⓓ She enjoys going to the dentist and pulling weeds.

8. When the 21st century began, where was the world's tallest building located?

Ⓐ the U.S.A.   Ⓒ Malaysia

Ⓑ Dubai   Ⓓ Kuala Lumpur

Part 3: Search "Reaching New Heights" to find one example of each of the following. Then write the number of the source in which you located this information.

9. word meaning "in an unbroken sequence" _____   Source #: _____

10. word meaning "accomplish or bring about" _____   Source #: _____

Reaching New Heights *(cont.)*

Name: _____

Part 4: Refer back to the sources to answer these questions.

11. Which five buildings were the tallest in the world for the longest periods of time during the 100-year period from 1913–2013? The first row has been filled in for you. (**Hint:** If two buildings were the tallest for an equal length of time, then list the buildings in chronological order.)

#	Name of Building	From	To	Length of Time
1.	Empire State Building	1931	1972	41 years
2.				
3.				
4.				
5.				

12. Put the following events in chronological order. Put a "1" next to the event that happened first. Put a "5" next to the event that happened last. On the last line, add a sixth event that you find in one of the sources. This event will have happened after all of the others listed.

_____ Suzy Walsham won her first Empire State Building Run-Up.

_____ The world's tallest building was built in Chicago.

_____ The world's tallest building was built in Taiwan.

_____ Thomas Dold won his third Empire State Building Run-Up.

_____ The Empire State Building Run-Up was first run.

___6___ _____

13. The title of this unit is "Reaching New Heights." Using what you have learned from all of the sources, name at least two different ways in which this title is appropriate. Use complete sentences.

_____

_____

_____

_____

_____

_____

_____

_____

Honoring Olympic Heroes

Read each source below. Then complete the activities on pages 57–58.

Source 1

Ken cleared his throat and began speaking. "For my speech on Olympic heroes, I have chosen Luz Long. You may not know who that is, and that is why I'm here to tell you why I think 'Luz Long' should be a household name."

Ken paused and then continued, "Luz Long was a great German long jumper who competed in the 1936 Olympic Games. These Games were held in Long's home country. At that time, Germany was led by Adolf Hitler and his Nazi Party. They believed that people who came from a specific northern European race were superior to people from other races. Within three years, the Nazi Party would use these beliefs to launch attacks on many peoples, races, and countries. This led to World War II.

"Adolf Hitler was in attendance at the Games when Long competed against other athletes, including the great Jesse Owens. Owens was an African American, one of the races the Nazi Party considered to be inferior. Owens was an incredible athlete, but he was in danger of being disqualified. On his first two long jumps, his foot had touched the foul line. This was not allowed. Long could see that Owens was upset. Despite being watched by Hitler, Long went over to Owens and offered him friendly advice. He told Owens to jump from a few inches behind the line. His jumps were plenty long, and he didn't need to get so close to the line to win. Owens took Long's advice, and he went on to win the gold medal. Long won the silver. The two athletes talked and congratulated one another as they walked off the field. Later, Owens said about Long, 'It took a lot of courage for him to befriend me in front of Hitler.'

"Sadly, Long died in 1943 while fighting for the German army in World War II."

Source 2

The Pierre de Coubertin Medal for Sportsmanship

- named for Pierre de Coubertin, a French historian who founded the International Olympic Committee (IOC) in 1894
- given by the IOC to athletes who have shown honorable sportsmanship while competing in Olympic events

Source 3

LEMIEUX HONORED

Canadian sailor Lawrence Lemieux received one of the highest Olympic honors today when he was awarded the Pierre de Coubertin Medal for Sportsmanship. Lemieux is only the fourth Olympic athlete to be bestowed this medal, which is given to those who exemplify the spirit of sportsmanship in Olympic events. Past winners have been Eugenio Monti of Italy (in 1964), Luz Long of Germany (in 1964), and Karl Heinz Klee of Austria (in 1977).

Lemieux earned this honor by saving two sailors from Singapore whose ship had tipped over during a race. Lemieux spotted the capsized boat and changed his course to provide assistance. In doing so, he gave up a chance to win an Olympic medal. He had been in second place when this incident occurred. He put the safety of others in front of his desire to compete and win. By the time the sailors were safe and Lemieux had reentered the race, he was only able to finish in 22nd place. His courage and quick thinking, however, saved two fellow athletes from a life-threatening situation.

Honoring Olympic Heroes *(cont.)*

Name: _____

Part 1: Read each idea. Which source gives you this information? Fill in the correct bubble for each source. (Note: More than one bubble may be filled in for each idea.)

Information	Sources ➡	1	2	3
1. Pierre de Coubertin was a French historian.		○	○	○
2. An Olympic medal was named for Pierre de Coubertin.		○	○	○
3. Luz Long was a German athlete.		○	○	○
4. Luz Long was awarded a Pierre de Coubertin Medal.		○	○	○

Part 2: Fill in the bubble next to the best answer to each question.

5. Look again at the title of this unit. Which words from this title share the same beginning sound?

   Ⓐ "Honoring" and "Olympic"   Ⓒ all of them do

   Ⓑ "Honoring" and "Heroes"   Ⓓ none of them do

6. What kind of person would the term "household name" (from Source 1) usually describe?

   Ⓐ a person whose name is written in most houses

   Ⓑ a person whose name is known by most people

   Ⓒ a person whose house is famous and often visited

   Ⓓ a person whose house is full of Olympic medals

7. Which word from Source 3 is the most similar to the words "given" or "presented"?

   Ⓐ bestowed   Ⓒ occurred

   Ⓑ earned   Ⓓ received

8. How many years passed from the creation of the IOC to the first time the Pierre de Coubertin Medal was awarded to an athlete?

   Ⓐ about 40   Ⓒ about 70

   Ⓑ about 60   Ⓓ about 100

Part 3: Search "Honoring Olympic Heroes" to find examples of words with the following meanings. Then write the number of the source in which you located this information.

9. "better than" _____   Source #: _____

10. "show an example of" _____   Source #: _____

Honoring Olympic Heroes (cont.)

Name: _____

Part 4: Refer back to the sources, and use complete sentences to answer these questions.

11. Use information given in the sources to fill in the timeline below. Add one event from each time period shown. The first event is written in for you.

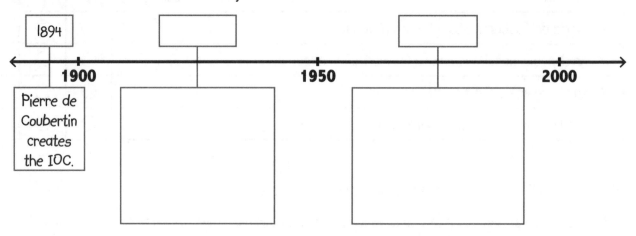

12. Compare and contrast the Olympic stories of Luz Long and Lawrence Lemieux. As you give details about each athlete's deeds and sacrifices, tell how they are the same or different.

_____

_____

_____

_____

_____

_____

_____

_____

_____

_____

_____

_____

13. On a separate piece of paper, retell the story of Luz Long and Jesse Owens from the perspective of either athlete. Use the first-person voice (*I, me,* etc.).

A Storm with Your Name

Read each source below. Then complete the activities on pages 60–61.

Source 1

The Saffir-Simpson scale was developed in 1971 by engineer Herb Saffir and meteorologist Bob Simpson. It categorized tropical storms and hurricanes based on the intensity of their sustained wind speeds.

Type of Storm	Wind Speeds
Tropical Storm	39–73 mph
Hurricane (Category 1)	74–95 mph
Hurricane (Category 2)	96–110 mph
Hurricane (Category 3)	111–129 mph
Hurricane (Category 4)	130–156 mph
Hurricane (Category 5)	> 157 mph

Source 2

The National Hurricane Center tracks all of the storms over the Atlantic Ocean. If a storm's winds sustain an intensity of 40 miles per hour (mph) or greater, the storm is named. Here is how:

There are six lists of 21 names each. Each list is alternated every six years. For example, the list that was used in 2000 is also used in 2006, 2012, 2018, and so on.

Each name on a list starts with a different letter of the alphabet. However, names beginning with Q, U, X, Y, or Z are never used. The storms are named in alphabetical and chronological order. This means that the first storm of the season is given the name that begins with "A", the second is given a name starting with "B", and so on. For example, the first major storm of 2010 was named Hurricane Alex, and the second major storm was called Tropical Storm Bonnie.

The same list is used every six years. A name will be retired, however, if a storm that has been given that name is particularly devastating. That name will be removed from the list and never used again. For example, 2012's Hurricane Sandy caused $68 billion in damages and killed 286 people. Therefore, the name Sandy has been retired and replaced by another name that begins with the letter "S."

Source 3

The year was 2018, and Sara Stormer wanted to crawl inside a hole and hide. Her whole town was bracing for one of the strongest hurricanes in history. Living on the southeastern coast of the United States, Sara had already lived through a few hurricane scares in her 14 years. But this hurricane was different. This hurricane had her name.

For several days now, Sara heard cries of "Hurricane Sara is coming! Get out of town before Sara hits! Sara is the worst thing that's ever happened to us!" Sara—the person, not the hurricane—couldn't help but feel awful. She wanted this whole hurricane thing to blow over and go away. She didn't think her little town could sustain this level of anxiety any longer. She wanted everyone to be safe and happy. She also wanted her name back.

Source 4

Top 10 Costliest Hurricanes (from 2004–2013)

Name	Year	Category	Cost (in Billions)	Deaths
Katrina	2005	5	$125	1,883
Sandy	2012	3	$68	286
Ike	2008	4	$37.5	195
Wilma	2005	5	$29.3	23
Ivan	2004	5	$23.3	124
Irene	2011	3	$16.6	56
Charley	2004	4	$15.1	40
Rita	2005	5	$12	62
Frances	2004	4	$9.85	49
Jeanne	2004	3	$7.66	3,035

A Storm with Your Name (cont.)

Name: _____

Part 1: Read each idea. Which source gives you this information? Fill in the correct bubble for each source. (Note: More than one bubble may be filled in for each idea.)

Information	Sources ➡	1	2	3	4
1. Hurricanes cannot begin with the letter "Z."		○	○	○	○
2. Hurricanes can begin with the letter "S."		○	○	○	○
3. Hurricane Sandy caused a lot of damage in 2012.		○	○	○	○
4. A Category 5 hurricane sustains winds of over 157 mph.		○	○	○	○

Part 2: Fill in the bubble next to the best answer to each question.

5. Which of these names could a hurricane in the year 2024 have?

Ⓐ Ivan

Ⓑ Isaac

Ⓒ Ulysses

Ⓓ Xavier

6. Which word from the sources means "continued without interruption over an extended period of time"?

Ⓐ retired

Ⓑ sustained

Ⓒ alternated

Ⓓ categorized

7. What percentage of the storms listed in Source 4 occurred in 2005?

Ⓐ 10%   Ⓑ 20%   Ⓒ 30%   Ⓓ 40%

8. Which of the following can you **not** infer from the information given in the sources?

Ⓐ Hurricanes often affect the southeastern coast of the U.S.

Ⓑ Hurricane Sara will be one of the costliest storms ever.

Ⓒ "Sara" replaced "Sandy" on one of the lists of hurricane names.

Ⓓ Hurricane Sandy sustained winds of at least 111 mph.

Part 3: Search "A Storm with Your Name" to find one example of each of the following. For each, you are given the number of the source in which this information is located.

9. an adverb with five syllables (2) _____

10. a pair of homophones (3) _____

Name: _____

Part 4: Refer back to the sources, and use complete sentences to answer these questions.

11. Put the hurricanes from the chart in Source 4 in chronological (time) order. On the lines below, explain how you were able to do this when you are only given the years (not the month) when these hurricanes occurred.

1st _____   6th _____

2nd _____   7th _____

3rd _____   8th _____

4th _____   9th _____

5th _____   10th _____

_____

_____

12. Study the information given in the chart in Source 4 and make two more observations based on the data (one is given for you). Give specific examples to back up your conclusions.

❶ None of the costliest hurricanes occurred in 2006, 2007, 2009, or 2010. _____

❷ _____

_____

❸ _____

_____

13. Imagine sharing your name with a devastating hurricane. How would that make you feel? Rewrite Source 3, but use a first-person voice this time. Use your name for the name of the coming storm.

_____

_____

_____

_____

_____

_____

_____

About Alike Animals

Read each source below and on page 63. Then complete the activities on pages 64–65.

Source 1

Going to the zoo with Misha is like having my own tour guide. She knows a lot about animals—and she is very eager to share her animal knowledge. So, I really opened up a can of worms when I said, "Ooh, look at that alligator over there. He looks mean."

"That is no alligator," said Misha. "See how a tooth from its lower jaw is sticking out of its mouth? That's the simplest way to know that you are looking at a crocodile."

I nodded as Misha continued. "People often mistake certain animals for other animals. For example, you might think turtles are the same as tortoises. They're not. Turtles need to live near water, while tortoises live on land and don't swim. It's kind of the same with frogs and toads. If you see one living near water, it's probably a frog."

Just then, I saw a sign with a gorilla on it. "Let's go that way. Monkeys are fascinating to watch."

Misha's eyes widened and she gasped, "Did you just call that gorilla a monkey? Allison, apes are very different from monkeys. For starters, apes are more intelligent, and they don't have tails. Wow, I have a lot to teach you."

Source 2

Prepositions are used to show a person or object's relationship to other things. Prepositions often answer questions such as *where, when, how,* and *why.*

Here are some common prepositions:

about, above, across, after, along, around, as, at, before, behind, below, beside, between, by, except, for, from, in, inside, into, of, on, outside, over, past, since, through, to, toward, under, up, with, without

A prepositional phrase starts with a preposition and ends with a word that is the object of the phrase.

Examples:

▶ <u>over</u> the rainbow
▶ <u>through</u> the door
▶ <u>from</u> my aunt
▶ <u>to</u> her
▶ <u>without</u> a sound

Source 3

I couldn't believe my eyes. "This picture is all wrong," I said to my best friends, Amy and Kay. "Who drew this?"

Amy squinted at the card that was pinned beside the picture. "It says that the painter's name is Artie Lyson. I kind of like it. The colors are beautiful."

"Me, too," said Kay. "It's got a lot of detail. Did you see that lion behind the tree? It's so life-like."

I shook my head, "It's not the art that bothers me. I just think the picture is unrealistic. You would never find all of these animals in one place at the same time. This artist is even showing a gorilla feeding a monkey. Those are two completely different animals!"

Amy and Kay nodded, but they might have been humoring me. They're probably thinking, "There goes Julie again, taking things too seriously. Why doesn't she just relax and enjoy the pretty picture?"

About Alike Animals *(cont.)*

Outside the Zoo

by Artie Lyson

Name: _____

Part 1: Read each idea. Which source gives you this information? Fill in the correct bubble for each source. (Note: More than one bubble may be filled in for each idea.)

Information	Sources ➡	1	2	3	4
1. The word *about* can be a preposition.		○	○	○	○
2. Gorillas are not the same as monkeys.		○	○	○	○
3. There is a painting called *Outside the Zoo*.		○	○	○	○
4. There is an artist named Artie Lyson.		○	○	○	○

Part 2: Fill in the bubble next to the best answer to each question.

5. What is the part of speech of the underlined word in this sentence: "There goes Julie again, taking things too <u>seriously</u>."

 Ⓐ noun   Ⓑ verb   Ⓒ adjective   Ⓓ adverb

6. Which underlined word is not used as a preposition in these sentences.

 Ⓐ Tim walked <u>down</u> the sidewalk.

 Ⓑ He walked <u>past</u> a yellow house.

 Ⓒ In the <u>past</u>, he knew someone who lived there.

 Ⓓ Tim knocked <u>on</u> the door to see if anyone was home.

7. In Source 1, the narrator says that she "opened up a can of worms." Which answer best describes what this idiom means?

 Ⓐ She tripped over a container of worms, and it opened.

 Ⓑ She mistook a certain animal for another animal.

 Ⓒ She created a situation that could be unpleasant.

 Ⓓ She eagerly shared her animal knowledge.

8. Which animal is mentioned in Source 1 but not pictured in Source 4?

 Ⓐ lion   Ⓑ monkey   Ⓒ alligator   Ⓓ crocodile

Part 3: Search "About Alike Animals" to find words with the following definitions. Then write the number of the source in which you located this information.

9. "wanting to do something very much" _____ Source #: _____

10. "looked with eyes partially closed" _____ Source #: _____

Name: _____

Part 4: Refer back to the sources, and use complete sentences to answer these questions.

11. Search Source 3 to find a sentence that contains at least three prepositional phrases. In the box below, quote that sentence. Underline each prepositional phrase.

12. Which character from Source 3 is most like Misha? Give the character's name and explain your answer.

_____

_____

_____

_____

_____

_____

_____

_____

13. Look again at Source 4. Write one sentence each about four more of the animals in the picture. Use a prepositional phrase in each sentence to describe where the animal is in relation to another animal or object. Underline the prepositional phrase. An example is given.

① *The lion is <u>behind the tree.</u>* _____

② _____

③ _____

④ _____

⑤ _____

We Can All Agree

Read each source below. Then complete the activities on pages 67–68.

Source 1

The good news is that Dad is taking Penny and me to the movies. The bad news is that we have to make a decision. This isn't always easy in our house.

Penny loves movies about animals, and I love anything to do with science fiction. Dad will watch anything, I suppose. His main concern is that our movie outing fits into his busy schedule.

Penny says, "I've been wanting to see *The Tails of Two Kitties* forever! Please, please, please! Let's see that one." I laugh, because Penny's jumping up and down, and because she's dressed head-to-toe in bright green. It's St. Patrick's Day, and Penny looks like a little leprechaun.

Dad looks at the listing of showtimes for movies at the Silver Screen Cinema, and then slowly shakes his head. "I'm sorry, Penny. It starts at 2:30, and it's 123 minutes long. We need to be home by 4:30 so I can get the roast in the oven."

Secretly, I'm happy to hear this, because I don't want to see that movie. Penny pouts, though. That is when I make a suggestion. "How about *Moose on Mars III*? *Moose on Mars I* was really funny, and *Moose on Mars II* wasn't bad."

Penny perks up, "A moose is an animal."

After checking the listing again, Dad said, "That's a good idea, Brian. The timing should work. Do we all agree on seeing *Moose on Mars III*?"

Source 2

running time — the length of a movie in minutes, from beginning to end

Source 3

Moose on Mars
III

"Bruce is loose . . . again."

Written and Directed by Anthony Antler

Description: This hilarious film begins where *Moose on Mars II* ended. Now that Bruce the Moose has saved his Martian moose colony, he must learn to deal with his instant fame. Meanwhile, a new evil threat emerges, and it's everybody's favorite moose to the rescue.

Running Time: 77 minutes

Source 4

Silver Screen Cinema
This ticket good for one admission to

MOOSE ON MARS III

Theater #
3

Start Time
3:00

March 17, 2017

We Can All Agree (cont.)

Name: _____

Part 1: Read each piece of information. Which movie from the sources does it describe? Fill in the correct bubble. (Note: In some cases, both bubbles may be filled in.) If the information does not describe either movie, fill in the "Neither" column.

Information Movie ➡	*The Tails of Two Kitties*	*Moose on Mars III*	Neither
1. This movie features animal characters.	○	○	○
2. This movie takes place on another planet.	○	○	○
3. This movie has the later starting time.	○	○	○
4. This movie is over two hours long.	○	○	○

Part 2: Fill in the bubble next to the best answer to each question.

5. Whose name is not given in the sources?

    Ⓐ the main character in *Moose on Mars III*   Ⓒ the writer of *Moose on Mars III*

    Ⓑ the villain in *Moose on Mars III*   Ⓓ the director of *Moose on Mars III*

6. Look at the information given in Source 4. Which of the following is **not** a clue that tells you this is a stub from the movie Penny, Brian, and Dad saw?

    Ⓐ the number of the theater   Ⓒ the start time of the movie

    Ⓑ the name of the movie   Ⓓ the date on the ticket

7. Which source would most likely come from a glossary?

    Ⓐ Source 1   Ⓒ Source 3

    Ⓑ Source 2   Ⓓ Source 4

8. Which of these quotes from Source 1 does **not** show an example of an emotional reaction.

    Ⓐ "Penny's jumping up and down"   Ⓒ "Penny pouts"

    Ⓑ "Penny looks like a little leprechaun"   Ⓓ "Penny perks up"

Part 3: Search "We Can All Agree" to find a synonym for each of the following words. (The part of speech is given in parentheses.) Then write the number of the source in which you located each simile.

9. "funny" (adjective) _____ Source #: _____

10. "worry" (noun) _____ Source #: _____

We Can All Agree (cont.)

Name: _____

Part 4: Refer back to the sources, and use complete sentences to answer questions #12 and #13.

11. Silver Screen Cinema is known for starting their movies right on time. Use this information to help you complete the chart below.

	The Tails of Two Kitties	*Moose on Mars III*
Start Time		
Running Time		
Ending Time		

12. The unit is titled "We Can All Agree." For each family member, give at least one reason why he or she would agree to see *Moose on Mars III*.

_____

_____

_____

_____

_____

13. Source 1 is written in first person from the perspective of Brian. Write a short retelling of Source 1, but this time from the perspective of either Penny or Dad.

_____

_____

_____

_____

_____

_____

_____

_____

_____

A Way Across

Read each source below. Then complete the activities on pages 70–71.

Source 1

trans-

prefix

across, beyond, to the other side of

Source 2

In the United States today, transcontinental travel is fairly quick and very common. Cars, trucks, and airplanes constantly carry people and goods from coast to coast. This was not always the case, of course. Before air travel was possible and before a complex system of highways was built, the railroads were the only means to carry large numbers of people or goods long distances over land. And before May 10, 1869, there was no single railroad that spanned the entire country. This all changed on that day when the final spike was driven into the ground, completing the First Transcontinental Railroad. On that day, the Central Pacific Railroad Company (building east from California) met up with Union Pacific Railroad Company (building west from Iowa). This meeting took place in Promontory Summit in the Utah Territory. A ceremony took place there. A golden spike was used to join the two railroad lines and complete the historic route. In an instant, the time it took to travel across the United States was reduced from six months to just one week.

Source 3

May 10, 1869 – History was made today. This magnificent land in which I live just grew both greater and smaller with a few strikes of a hammer. It was an enormous feat, but the transcontinental railroad is now complete. Today, the final spike was driven into the ground.

A special golden spike was used for the occasion. On its top were the words, "The last Spike." At least a thousand people were gathered there to witness this historic occasion. When the ceremony was complete, the golden spike was replaced by an iron one. Then a telegraph operator sent a one-word message across the land in every direction. The word was "DONE." I can only imagine the cheers that erupted when people all across this great land heard the news.

Source 4

telegraph

from the Greek roots *tele* ("far") and *graph* ("writing")

The telegraph was an early communication device that used wires and electricity to transmit messages over long distances. Messages were sent in a series of dots and dashes named Morse code. This code could be translated into letters and words.

The telegraph was invented in the 1830s, about 40 years before the invention of the telephone. Before the telegraph, there were no methods available for sending messages quickly across vast distances.

Name: _____

Part 1: Read each idea. Which source gives you this information? Fill in the correct bubble for each source. (Note: More than one bubble may be filled in for each idea.)

Information	Sources ➡	1	2	3	4
1. The Transcontinental Railroad was completed in 1869.		○	○	○	○
2. The Transcontinental Railroad was completed in Utah Territory.		○	○	○	○
3. The Transcontinental Railroad was finished with a golden spike.		○	○	○	○
4. The golden spike was replaced almost immediately.		○	○	○	○

Part 2: Fill in the bubble(s) next to the best answer(s) to each question.

5. Which of these words from the sources means "went across"?

Ⓐ spanned   Ⓑ translated   Ⓒ historic   Ⓓ vast

6. Which of the sources could be an example of historical fiction?

Ⓐ Source 1   Ⓑ Source 2   Ⓒ Source 3   Ⓓ Source 4

7. From the information given, which of the following can you infer about Utah in 1869.

Ⓐ It was a territory—not a state—at that time.

Ⓑ It was east of Iowa.

Ⓒ It was east of California.

Ⓓ It was where the telegraph was invented.

8. From the information given, which of the following statements can you infer are true about the telephone?

Ⓐ It was invented in the 1830s.

Ⓑ It was invented in the 1870s.

Ⓒ It hadn't been invented when the First Transcontinental Railroad was completed.

Ⓓ Its Greek root words mean "far sound."

Part 3: Search "A Way Across" to find one example of each of the following. Then write the number of the source in which you located this information.

9. the name of a decade _____ Source #: _____

10. the name of an occupation _____ Source #: _____

A Way Across (cont.)

Name: _____

Part 4: Refer back to the sources, and use complete sentences to answer these questions.

11. How does the title "A Way Across" appropriately describe both the telegraph and a transcontinental railroad? Use evidence from the sources to support your answer.

_____

_____

_____

_____

_____

_____

12. In Source 3, the narrator says that as a result of the transcontinental railroad, the land in which he lives "just grew both greater and smaller." What do you think he means by that? How could something become greater *and* smaller?

_____

_____

_____

_____

_____

_____

13. In Source 3, the narrator mentions that news of the railroad's completion was instantly sent by telegraph all across the nation. Compare and contrast how news of the event was spread back then to how news of an event is spread now.

_____

_____

_____

_____

_____

_____

Words Made from Myths

Read each source below and on page 73. Then complete the activities on pages 74–75.

Source 1

Many words have their roots in Ancient Greek mythology. The chart below lists a few of these words and explains their origins.

Word	Figure of Speech	Pronunciation	Meaning	Named After	Why
atlas	noun	(at-lus)	a collection of maps	Atlas	Atlas led a struggle against the gods, and as punishment, he was forced to support the heavens on his shoulders for all of eternity.
echo	noun, verb	(eh-ko)	sound(s) that bounces off an object and comes back to the speaker	Echo	Echo loved the sound of her own voice and often distracted the goddess Hera with long stories. Hera punished her by taking away her voice. Echo was only able to repeat the exact words that were spoken to her.
Herculean	adjective	(her-kyoo-lee-un)	requiring great strength or effort	Hercules	Hercules is the Roman name for a Greek hero who was famous for his great strength and courage. Among his many feats, Hercules defeated a nine-headed snake named Hydra and captured a vicious, three-headed, dog-like creature named Cerberus.
narcissistic	adjective	(nar-si-sis-tik)	having an unhealthy interest in oneself and one's own physical beauty	Narcissus	Narcissus was known for being attractive, and he was overly proud of the effect his beauty had on other people. A god led Narcissus to a pool of water, where he caught sight of his reflection. He fell so in love with the image he saw that he was unable leave his spot beside the pool. He stayed looking at his reflection until he died.
Sisyphean	adjective	(si-sif-ee-un)	describes something (like a task) that can never be completed and is a source of unending frustration	Sisyphus	Sisyphus was a dishonest king whose punishment by the gods was to roll a giant boulder up a steep hill. Every time Sisyphus approached the top of the hill, the boulder would roll back down, and he would have to begin again. This series of events repeated forever.
tantalize	verb	(tan-tuh-lize)	to tease with the promise of something that one can never have	Tantalus	Tantalus is a figure from Greek mythology who committed such acts as stealing from the gods and murdering his own son. As punishment, the gods forced Tantalus to stand in a pool of water under a fruit tree. Every time he reached down to drink, the water receded. Every time he reached up to grab fruit, the tree's branches raised the fruit so that it was just out of reach.

Source 2

allusion

In writing, an allusion is a brief reference to a person, place, idea, or thing from culture, history, mythology, literature, etc. Usually, the allusion is not explained. Instead, the reader is expected to understand the meaning and origin of the reference.

Example #1: Upon seeing the class grades, Ben blurted, "Who's the Einstein who got an A+ on the test?"

Meaning: This is an allusion to Albert Einstein, a physicist who is known for being a genius.

Example #2: Bob said, "What's wrong with Mike? He looks like he's carrying the weight of the world on his shoulders."

Meaning: This is an allusion to Atlas from Greek mythology. His punishment for battling the gods was to hold up the heavens for all of time.

Source 3

Source 4

Imagine hunting over great distances in the dark of night for tiny treats that are nearly impossible to see. For humans, such a Sisyphean task would leave us tantalized and unsatisfied. But for bats, it's all in a night's work.

You see, many species of bats have developed a special ability to use sound waves to hunt at night. It's called *echolocation*, and insects and other targets don't have a chance against it. The word *echolocation* tells you exactly what it means: bats (along with some other animals, like toothed whales) use echoes to locate their prey. An echo occurs when a sound wave travels a distance, meets an object, and bounces back off that object. We can observe this effect when we call out across a large canyon or call down a deep well. Unlike these echoes, the echoes that bats hear bouncing off of bugs are not sounds that we can hear. They are too high-pitched. Not only can bats hear these echoes, but they can use them to determine where an object is, how big it is, and in which direction it is moving. All that is left at that point is for the bat to swoop in and grab a tasty meal.

Words Made from Myths (cont.)

Name: _____

Part 1: Read each idea. Which source gives you this information? Fill in the correct bubble for each source. (Note: More than one bubble may be filled in for each idea.)

Information	Sources ➡	1	2	3	4
1. According to myth, Hercules battled a creature named Hydra.		○	○	○	○
2. According to myth, Atlas was forced to hold up the heavens.		○	○	○	○
3. According to myth, Echo was in love with the sound of her voice.		○	○	○	○
4. Echoes occur when sounds bounce off objects and come back.		○	○	○	○

Part 2: Fill in the bubble(s) next to the best answer(s) to each question.

5. Which source illustrates an allusion to the myth of Narcissus?

Ⓐ Source 1   Ⓑ Source 2   Ⓒ Source 3   Ⓓ Source 4

6. Which of the following statements are true about Echo and Narcissus?

Ⓐ Both were in love with the sounds of their voices.

Ⓑ Both were in love with something about themselves.

Ⓒ Both are figures in Greek mythology.

Ⓓ Both died while staring at their own reflections.

7. In which of the following sentences is a form of the word *echo* used as a verb?

Ⓐ I could hear the <u>echoes</u> of our voices from across the canyon.

Ⓑ Throughout the night, the bat used <u>echoes</u> to locate his meals.

Ⓒ That parrot <u>echoes</u> my every word, and it's driving me crazy.

Ⓓ <u>Echo's</u> love of her own voice led to her punishment by the gods.

8. Source 1 gives information about six words that have their roots in Greek mythology. What fraction of these words contains more than two syllables? Fill in the circle for all correct answers.

Ⓐ $\frac{4}{6}$ Ⓑ $\frac{3}{6}$ Ⓒ $\frac{1}{2}$ Ⓓ $\frac{2}{3}$

Part 3: Search "Words Made From Myths" to find words with the following meanings. Then write the number of the source in which you located this information.

9. "moved back or farther away" _____ Source #: _____

10. "excessively cruel or violent" _____ Source #: _____

Words Made from Myths (cont.)

Name: _____

Part 4: Refer back to the sources, and use complete sentences to answer questions #11 and #13.

11. The author of Source 4 uses the words *echo* and *Sisyphean*. One of these words is used as an allusion to Greek mythology, and the other is not. Tell which is which, and give evidence to support your answer.

_____

_____

_____

_____

_____

_____

_____

12. Using the three panels below, create a cartoon about the myth of Sisyphus. You can make your cartoon silly, serious, or anything in between.

13. The gods of Greek mythology handed out a lot of punishments, and some of them were very inventive. Of the punishments detailed in Source 1, which one do you think is the most inventive or interesting? Why?

_____

_____

_____

_____

_____

_____

_____

Which "Sound" Do You See?

Read each source below. Then complete the activities on pages 77–78.

Source 1

sound *(noun)*

1. the sensation perceived by the sense of hearing

   The alarm clock made a loud, buzzing <u>sound</u>.

2. a long passage of water connecting two larger bodies of water

   Øresund, or "The <u>Sound</u>" as it is called, connects the Baltic Sea to the North Sea and is one of the busiest waterways in the world.

Source 2

sound *(verb)*

1. to cause something to make a sound

   They were taught to <u>sound</u> the fire alarm at the first sign of smoke.

2. to convey an impression when heard

   "Don't <u>sound</u> so worried," said Mark's mother.

Source 3

sound *(adjective)*

1. having no flaw or defect

   Even after the earthquake, the building's foundation remained <u>sound</u>.

2. sensible, wise

   Todd's uncle gave him some <u>sound</u> advice about money.

3. severe

   After the 56–0 loss, the coach admitted, "That was a <u>sound</u> beating."

Source 4

sound *(adverb)*

1. thoroughly and completely

   After hours of crying, the toddler finally fell <u>sound</u> asleep.

Source 5

The troop of soldiers began to cross the old, wooden footbridge. Even over the sound of pounding feet, ominous cracks and creaks could be heard. Without hesitation, the troop leader made the decision to sound his whistle and shout, "Halt!" At once, all noise ceased, save the sound of wind on the water below.

"This bridge needs to be inspected," shouted the leader. "If it breaks, we'll all end up in the sound, which does not sound like a good time to me."

The troop's head engineer began to inspect the bridge. He was known for being thorough and for displaying sound judgment in these situations. After 10 minutes of inspection and after several sound shakings of the bridge's main supports, he spoke. "There are a few weak boards, but the overall structure is sound. It is safe to cross."

"That's good enough for me," hollered the leader. "Let's go. It's been a long night. The sooner we get to camp, the sooner we can all be sound asleep."

Which "Sound" Do You See? (cont.)

Name: _____

Part 1: Look at the way *sound* is used in each sentence. Which source gives you an example of *sound* being used in this way? Fill in the correct bubble to name the source. (Note: Source 5 is not one of the answers available in this section.)

Information	Sources ➡	1	2	3	4
1. Felix fell sound asleep despite his noisy neighbors.		○	○	○	○
2. Our coaches don't sound happy about last night's loss.		○	○	○	○
3. That trumpet player is not making a good sound.		○	○	○	○
4. Cam came up with a sound solution to our problem.		○	○	○	○

Part 2: Fill in the bubble next to the best answer to each question.

5. Based on the information given, which word would **not** be used to describe the engineer in Source 5?

Ⓐ careful   Ⓒ incautious

Ⓑ cautious   Ⓓ rigorous

6. Which of the following words from Source 5 is a compound word?

Ⓐ inspection   Ⓒ wooden

Ⓑ footbridge   Ⓓ judgment

7. Based on the information given, one of the world's busiest waterways lies between these two countries.

Ⓐ North Sea and Baltic Sea   Ⓒ United States and Mexico

Ⓑ Denmark and Sweden   Ⓓ *none of the above*

8. In which point of view and tense is Source 5 written?

Ⓐ first person, present tense   Ⓒ third person, present tense

Ⓑ first person, past tense   Ⓓ third person, past tense

Part 3: Search "Which 'Sound' Do You See?" to find one example of each of the following. The first letter of the word is given in parentheses. Then write the number of the source in which you located this information.

9. an antonym for "began" (c)_____ Source #: _____

10. a synonym for "threatening" (o)_____ Source #: _____

Name: _____

Part 4: Refer back to the sources, and use complete sentences to answer these questions.

11. Each quote from Source 5 listed below contains the word *sound*. For each use of the word *sound*, name its part of speech. Also write the definition number from Sources 1–4 that applies. As an example, the first one is done for you.

  A. "Even over the <u>sound</u> of pounding feet..." _____ noun, 1 _____

  B. "the troop leader made the decision to <u>sound</u> his whistle" _____

  C. "all noise ceased, save the <u>sound</u> of wind on the water" _____

  D. "If it breaks, we'll all end up in the <u>sound</u>" _____

  E. "which does not <u>sound</u> like a good time" _____

  F. "He was known for . . . displaying <u>sound</u> judgment" _____

  G. "after several <u>sound</u> shakings, he spoke. _____

  H. "the overall structure is <u>sound</u>. It is safe" _____

  I. "the sooner we can all be <u>sound</u> asleep." _____

12. Do you think the troop in Source 5 contains a lot of soldiers or just a few? What gives you this impression of the troop's size?

  _____

  _____

  _____

13. Like *sound*, each of the words in the box below has several meanings. Choose one, and write three different sentences that contain the word. In each sentence, the word must have a different meaning or be used in a different way.

fine	mean	mind	save	sink	well

  _____

  _____

  _____

  _____

  _____

  _____

What's in a Name?

Read each source below. Then complete the activities on pages 80–81.

Source 1

I used to think I was the only one in the New England area who spells my name K-I-M-I. I've never even read a book in which a character spelled her name that way. Then I met another Kimi. She moved here from Kentucky two years ago, and we became best friends.

Everyone calls us the "Kimi Twins" even though we don't look alike. I have long, straight, black hair. Kentucky Kimi has curly blond hair. My eyes are blue, and hers are green.

In fact, she and I are different in most ways. For example, my idea of a tasty breakfast is steak and eggs. Kimi would not touch that plate with a ten-foot pole. She's a vegetarian, so she does not eat meat. She mostly eats strange things like tofu and hummus. The other day she brought some fruit to school that I had never seen before. It was this brown, fuzzy, egg-shaped thing. When she cut it open, the insides were bright green with rows of tiny black seeds. I said, "You're going to be here all day trying to get those seeds out." But she just ate them! She called this exotic fruit a kiwi and offered me some. I said, "No, thank you. I'll stick with my ham sandwich."

Source 2

Delicious, Nutritious Kiwifruits!
3 for $1.00

- once known as Chinese gooseberries
- brought to the United States in 1959 from New Zealand
- named after the kiwi, New Zealand's national bird
- great source of fiber and Vitamin C
- The seeds are edible!

Source 3

Nature's Amazing Oddballs

The world is full of amazingly interesting creatures. For today's article, I give you . . . **the Kiwi**.

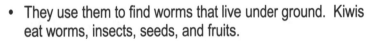

Kiwis have long beaks.

- They use them to find worms that live under ground. Kiwis eat worms, insects, seeds, and fruits.

- A kiwi's nostrils are at the end of its beak. This is unlike all other birds, and it gives kiwis a stronger sense of smell than other birds.

Kiwi cannot fly. They belong to the same family as other flightless birds—like ostriches and emus—but they are much smaller.

Kiwis are the size of chickens, but their eggs are six times as big as chicken eggs.

Kiwis come from New Zealand. In fact, they are that country's national bird.

What's in a Name? *(cont.)*

Name: _____

Part 1: Read each idea. Which source gives you this information? Fill in the correct bubble for each source. (Note: More than one bubble may be filled in for each idea.)

Information	Sources ➡	1	2	3
1. New Zealand's national bird is the kiwi.		○	○	○
2. Kiwifruits come from New Zealand.		○	○	○
3. For their size, kiwi birds have large eggs.		○	○	○
4. You can eat the seeds of a kiwifruit.		○	○	○

Part 2: Fill in the bubble(s) next to the best answer(s) to each question.

5. Which statement is true?

Ⓐ The Kimi Twins were named after each other.

Ⓑ The kiwifruit was named after the kiwi bird.

Ⓒ The kiwi bird was named after the kiwifruit.

Ⓓ New England was named after New Zealand.

6. The word *exotic* is used in Source 1 to describe a kiwifruit. Which of these words is an antonym of *exotic*?

Ⓐ unfamiliar   Ⓒ regular

Ⓑ strange   Ⓓ alien

7. In which of these places would you most likely find Source 2?

Ⓐ online advertisement   Ⓒ online encyclopedia

Ⓑ online dictionary   Ⓓ online thesaurus

8. From the information given in Source 1, you can infer that tofu and hummus _____.

Ⓐ do not taste good   Ⓒ are exotic to Kentucky Kimi

Ⓑ do not contain meat   Ⓓ are exotic to the narrator

Part 3: Search "What's in a Name?" to find one example of each of the following. Then write the number of the source in which you located this information.

9. a possessive common noun _____   Source #: _____

10. a possessive proper noun _____   Source #: _____

What's in a Name? *(cont.)*

Name: _____

Part 4: Refer back to the sources, and use complete sentences to answer these questions.

11. The author of Source 1 uses an idiom (a saying) to explain how strong Kentucky Kimi's feelings are about eating meat. In the box below, write the exact quote that contains this idiom.

```



```

12. Look at this incomplete analogy:

_____ are to **kiwis** as **kiwi eggs** are to **chicken eggs**.

Fill in the circle next to the word that best completes the analogy. Then on the lines below, explain what the completed analogy means.

Ⓐ kiwifruits   Ⓑ chickens   Ⓒ ostriches   Ⓓ nostrils

_____

_____

_____

_____

13. Source 1 is written from one Kimi's perspective. Write a paragraph from the other Kimi's perspective. Include details from the original story. Your new story can be about the first day the two Kimis met or about the day Kentucky Kimi brought a kiwifruit to school for lunch.

_____

_____

_____

_____

_____

_____

_____

_____

_____

_____

_____

Unit 24

When You're From

Read each source below and on page 83. Then complete the activities on pages 84–85.

Source 1

In Isaac's Time

a play by Casey Munson

Isaac Newton: You say you are from the future. How is this possible?

Casey: Where I'm from—or *when* I'm from—time travel is simple. Everybody does it. What I can't believe is that nobody has visited you before. My homework assignment was to travel back in time and observe someone from history. Who would be better to observe than one of the greatest scientists and mathematicians to ever live?

Isaac Newton: I've built telescopes and other instruments, but a time-travel device? Please explain how it works. You must be brilliant.

Casey: Not really. I got inside a machine. I pushed a button.

Isaac Newton: Surely, you must have some wisdom to impart to me. If you could share some mathematical knowledge or some law of science that is not yet in my grasp . . . I would be most grateful.

Casey: *(thinking long and hard)* Wait, I do know a math trick! It's a very special equation.

Isaac Newton: *(with interest)* I would like to hear it.

Casey: If you follow 12 simple steps and then tell me the number you come up with, I can tell you the date of your birth. Would you like me to show you?

Isaac Newton: *(with great enthusiasm)* Would I? That sounds amazing!

Casey: Begin by adding the number 18 to your birth month.

page 1

Source 2

Isaac In Our Time

by Cassie Munson

Many things can be said,
and this one's true:
A genius was born
December 25, 1642.

Isaac Newton was his name,
and he taught us so much
About physics and mathematics
and astronomy and such.

His theories on gravity
and how we see light
His three laws of motion,
all still known to be right.

Such an influential thinker,
brings this thought to mind:
What would he do
if he lived in our time?

❖ DECEMBER 1642 ❖

S	M	T	W	T	F	S
	1	2	3	4	5	6
7	8	9	10	11	12	13
14	15	16	17	18	19	20
21	22	23	24	25	26	27
28	29	30	31			

Source 3

The Birthday Equation

Step 1: First, add 18 to your birth month. (For example, if you were born in February, you would add 2 + 18.)

Step 2: Next, multiply by 25.

Step 3: Then, subtract 333.

Step 4: Multiply the resulting number by 8.

Step 5: Subtract 554.

Step 6: Divide the result by 2.

Step 7: Add your birth date. (For example, if you were born on May 12, you would add 12.)

Step 8: Multiply by 5.

Step 9: Add 692.

Step 10: Multiply by 20.

Step 11: Add only the last two digits of your birth year.

Step 12: Subtract 32,940.

The result will be a five- or six-digit number that will be your birthday. (Hint: Those with birthdays from January to September will get a five-digit number. Those with birthdays in October, November, or December will get a six-digit number.)

Examples (with the months and years underlined):

✳ If your final answer is <u>3</u>1,6<u>05</u>, your birthday is March 16, 2005.

✳ If your final answer is <u>10</u>0,9<u>07</u>, your birthday is October 9, 2007.

Source 4

Comparing Writing Categories
student handout for Mr. Mack's class

For your assignment, you will be asked to write about an important historical figure. You will also be asked to explore different writing genres. Choose one genre and one historical figure from the field of science. Some good choices for scientists are listed below. Here are the three writing categories to choose from:

- **Prose** is the language most often used when writing or speaking. Most writing that is meant to inform or explain is written in prose. Nonfiction articles and essays are prose, as are most fictional stories.

- **Poetry** often uses a minimum number of words to express feelings, describe moments, or paint word pictures. Poems often use elements such as rhythm, rhyme, patterns, and imagery.

- **Drama** is a story that is performed to an audience. A drama is often called a play, and it is written in a special form called a *script*. A script contains three main elements: the names of the characters (the people, animals, etc., in the story), the dialogue (the words spoken by the characters), and the stage directions (the actions of the characters).

Some historical figures from the field of science (listed alphabetically): Copernicus (born 1473), Marie Curie (born 1867), Charles Darwin (born 1809), Albert Einstein (born 1879), Galileo Galilei (born 1564), Stephen Hawking (born 1942), Isaac Newton (born 1642), Louis Pasteur (born 1822).

When You're From (cont.)

Name: _____

Part 1: Read each idea. Which source gives you this information? Fill in the correct bubble for each source. (Note: More than one bubble may be filled in for each idea.)

Information	Sources ➡	1	2	3	4
1. There is a math equation for figuring out a person's birthday.		○	○	○	○
2. Isaac Newton is an important historical figure in science.		○	○	○	○
3. Isaac Newton is an important historical figure in mathematics.		○	○	○	○
4. Isaac Newton was born on December 25, 1642.		○	○	○	○

Part 2: Fill in the bubble next to the best answer to each question.

5. On which day of the week was Isaac Newton born?

Ⓐ December 25

Ⓑ 1642

Ⓒ Tuesday

Ⓓ Thursday

6. If a person's answer to the birthday equation is 11,309, then on what day was that person born?

Ⓐ January 3, 2009

Ⓑ January 13, 2009

Ⓒ November 3, 2009

Ⓓ November 30, 2009

7. Which of the following is an example of a stage direction?

Ⓐ "(the words spoken by characters)"

Ⓑ "(listed alphabetically)"

Ⓒ "(with great enthusiasm)"

Ⓓ "(with the months and years underlined)"

8. What is the main theme of Source 2?

Ⓐ Isaac Newton was a scientist.

Ⓑ Isaac Newton described three laws of motion.

Ⓒ Isaac Newton was one of the most brilliant minds in history.

Ⓓ Isaac Newton could accomplish a lot if he were alive today.

Part 3: Search "When You're From" to find one example of each of the following. Then write the number of the source in which you located this information.

9. an adverb containing six syllables _____ Source #: _____

10. a five-letter synonym for "understanding" _____ Source #: _____

Part 4: Refer back to the sources to answer these questions.

11. Look at the eight scientists named in Source 4, and do the following three things:

    A. Name the percentage of them that were born in the 19th century? _____

    B. Explain how you came up with this answer.

    _____

    _____

    C. Write the names of the 19th-century scientists in chronological order by their year of birth.

    _____

    _____

12. Give at least three examples from the source that support the following claim: Source 1 is a work of fiction.

_____

_____

_____

_____

_____

_____

13. If the birthday equation works like it is supposed to, what number
will you come up with if you do the equation for your birthday?
(Answer this question before using the equation.) _____

Now use the equation for your birthday. Show your work in the box.
Did you come up with the number you gave in the previous answer? _____

Unit
25

Teaching the New Teacher

Read each source below and on page 87. Then complete the activities on pages 88–89.

Source 1

Principal Clark shook Mr. Tanner's hand and motioned to the only chair in her office. "Please have a seat," she said. "Welcome to Adams Elementary. We're happy to have you on our team. Thomas York says you're a great teacher."

Smiling, Mr. Tanner said, "I'll have to thank Principal York. That's quite a compliment. And I'm thrilled to be here. I can't wait to meet the class and get started."

"You're inheriting a great group of kids," replied Principal Clark. "I know Mrs. May is sad to be leaving them, but her baby is due any day now. You'll be taking over her class until the end of the year, and then Mrs. May will be back in August. That'll give her five full months of at-home time with her newborn."

PRINCIPAL CLARK

Principal Clark handed Mr. Tanner a packet of papers and continued speaking. "Here's a class roster with every student's name on it. We're a small school in a tiny town, so your class only has 10 students. Attached to the roster is a sheet on the different learning styles. I know you've taught before and are probably very familiar with this stuff, but it's a good idea to keep these learning styles in mind when you design your class lessons. Now let me tell you a little bit about the special students in your class. Ceci's family just moved here last month, and she's already a member of our Math Wizards program. Gaby is one of the younger students, but you wouldn't know it from her personality. She loves to dance and sing, and she's very outgoing. Daniel is a little more reserved, but he's an excellent writer. Jenny and Willow are inseparable. You'll see them jumping rope together or practicing gymnastics every day at recess. Speaking of close, the Tucker twins are rarely apart. They complement each other well. Andrew is great with numbers, and Allison has a way with words. What can I say about Jace Jordan? He designed the school logo you see on the front of our school. He did that when he was only seven years old! And then there's Quinton. His parents must have given him a drum set before he could walk, because he's a natural percussionist. He and Gaby should form a band together some day. Lastly, we have Pam. She walked right up to me the other day and said, 'I want to be a dendrologist when I grow up.' I had to look that word up to learn it's a person who studies trees! So don't worry if you catch Pam staring out of the window. She likes looking at the trees swaying in the breeze, and it seems to help her think more clearly. Well, that's the whole group. You're going to love being their teacher. Shall I introduce you to them now?"

Teaching the New Teacher *(cont.)*

Mrs. May, Room 6
Class Roster

Student	Nickname	DOB	Gender	Notes
Clayton, Quinton	—	12/29/06	male	return his drumsticks (in upper left desk drawer) each day after school
Garcia, Gabriella	Gaby	2/3/08	female	
Han, Jenny	—	12/16/07	female	must sit apart from Willow during lessons
Jordan, Jason	Jace	5/9/07	male	getting glasses soon; can't see board if he sits too far away
Leigh, Willow	—	11/11/07	female	see note Jenny Han
Muro, Cecilia	Ceci	3/16/08	female	excuse for Math Wizards program every day at 2:15; seat near door
Tucker, Allison	—	6/30/07	female	older than Andrew by six minutes!
Tucker, Andrew	—	6/30/07	male	
Wardlow, Pamela	Pam	11/22/06	female	speak to parents about explorer camp
Wayne, Daniel	—	1/1/08	male	prefers to sit in back of class

Adams Elementary School
Learning Styles

The following categories describe different types of learners. Most students fall into more than one category, but you might find that many students favor one certain type of learning above all others.

➤ **Linguistic:** learns best through language (words, writing)

➤ **Logical:** learns best through science and math (numbers, charts, and graphics)

➤ **Visual:** learns best through art, design, and shapes

➤ **Interpersonal:** learns best through an understanding of oneself; thinks deeply

➤ **Kinesthetic:** learns best through sports and movement

➤ **Musical:** learns best through tone, rhythm, and dance

➤ **Natural:** learns best through understanding the outside world

Name: _____

Part 1: Read each idea. Which source gives you this information? Fill in the correct bubble for each source. (Note: More than one bubble may be filled in for each idea.)

Information	Sources ➡	1	2	3
1. Adams Elementary is the name of a school.		◯	◯	◯
2. Jace Jordan is a student in Mrs. May's class.		◯	◯	◯
3. Jace Jordan designed his school's logo.		◯	◯	◯
4. The word *kinesthetic* is related to movement.		◯	◯	◯

Part 2: Fill in the bubble next to the best answer to each question.

5. In what order does Principal Clark describe Mrs. May's students to Mr. Tanner?

Ⓐ alphabetical order by first name

Ⓑ alphabetical order by last name

Ⓒ from youngest to oldest

Ⓓ from oldest to youngest

6. From the third paragraph in Source 1, you can infer that this meeting takes place in the month of _____.

Ⓐ March   Ⓒ April

Ⓑ May   Ⓓ August

7. In simplest terms, what fraction of the students in the class are boys?

Ⓐ $\frac{1}{2}$ Ⓑ $\frac{2}{5}$ Ⓒ $\frac{2}{10}$ Ⓓ $\frac{4}{10}$

8. Which of Mrs. May's students would most likely appreciate the previous question and get the answer correct?

Ⓐ Pam Wardlow   Ⓒ Ceci Muro

Ⓑ Jace Jordan   Ⓓ Daniel Wayne

Part 3: Search "Teaching the New Teacher" to find **homophones** with the following meanings. Then write the number of the source in which you located this information.

9. "to complete or make whole" _____ Source #: _____

10. "an expression of praise or admiration" _____ Source #: _____

Name: _____

Part 4: Refer back to the sources to answer these questions.

11. Create a pictograph for Mrs. May's class. Use the key to help you. Above each symbol you enter on the graph, write the name of the student it represents. The first one has been done for you.

🧍 = 1 student

students born in 2006	Quinton 🧍
students born in 2007	
students born in 2008	

12. Fill out a seating chart for Mrs. May's class. Be sure to keep in mind the particular needs of certain students, as described in the sources.

Front of Class

Window   Door

Back of Class

13. Complete the chart below. Name one student who would excel at each of the learning styles listed. In the "Why?" column, provide a quote from the sources that proves your answer.

Learning Style	Student Name	Why?
Kinesthetic		
Linguistic		
Naturalist		

Into and Out of Thin Air

Read each source below. Then complete the activities on pages 91–92.

Source 1

into thin air

Idiom: "vanish into thin air" (also, "disappear into thin air")

Meaning: to disappear, never to be seen again

---

out of thin air

Idiom: "appear out of thin air"

Meaning: suddenly and mysteriously appear

Source 2

The Water Cycle

Mr. Tanner's Class
Adams Elementary School, Room 6

Water does not come to Earth from other places. The water on Earth has always been here. It constantly gets used and reused. This is possible because of the water cycle. Water is always on the move. It moves from one place to another and from one form (solid, liquid, gas) to another.

There are four main stages of the water cycle:

1. **Evaporation** — During this stage, heat from the Sun causes water (in oceans, lakes, etc.) to evaporate (turn from a liquid into a gas). This gas is called water vapor, and it rises into the sky.

2. **Condensation** — As the water vapor in the air cools, it turns back into water droplets. The droplets form clouds in the sky.

3. **Precipitation** — As the droplets in the sky continue to condense, they become too heavy. It is called precipitation when the water falls back to the ground. It does this in many forms: rain, snow, sleet, hail.

4. **Collection** — When water falls to the ground, some of it ends up on land, where it nourishes plants and animals. The rest runs off the land and collects in oceans, lakes, rivers, and other bodies of water.

Source 3

Thomas Tanner was in a panic. His students were staring at him. He thought he had prepared well for this day, but when he tried to open his computer file on the water cycle, all of the artwork was missing. The visuals seemed to have vanished into thin air.

The previous evening, Thomas had drawn clouds, raindrops, and all of the other elements that illustrated just how the water cycle works. He had scanned them into his computer. Everything was there when he went to sleep last night, and now *poof*—it was all gone. How could this happen? How would his students understand the concept of the water cycle if there were no visuals to go with the words? Peter wiped a bead of sweet from his brow and made a split-second decision. Instead of interrupting class to redo his presentation, he began to teach the four main stages of the water cycle. He decided that he would ask his students to draw the illustrations based on the descriptions he provided.

Source 4

I sighed and got busy searching Mr. Tanner's computer for the "lost" artwork. I knew those files had to be somewhere. Data doesn't just disappear into thin air. Don't get me wrong—these teachers at Adams Elementary are great with kids, and they know their multiplication tables and dates in history. Technology is another story. Most of the teachers at this school are not exactly experts when it comes to computers. They hit the wrong button and accidentally delete something, and then the principal calls me in to help find it. I can retrieve most any file. Things rarely get lost. I know where to look. Then it appears as if I pull the missing data out of thin air, but really it is hiding in plain sight the whole time.

Into and Out of Thin Air (cont.)

Name: _____

Part 1: Read each idea. Which source gives you this information? Fill in the correct bubble for each source. (Note: More than one bubble may be filled in for each idea.)

Information	Sources ➡	1	2	3	4
1. Rain is a part of the water cycle.		○	○	○	○
2. Rain is a form of condensation.		○	○	○	○
3. Mr. Tanner is a teacher at Adams Elementary School.		○	○	○	○
4. Mr. Tanner's first name is Thomas.		○	○	○	○

Part 2: Fill in the bubble next to the best answer to each question.

5. Which of the sources is written in a first-person voice?

Ⓐ Source 1   Ⓒ Source 3

Ⓑ Source 2   Ⓓ Source 4

6. Which two words from Source 4 are homophones?

Ⓐ *sighed* and *sight*   Ⓒ *knew* and *new*

Ⓑ *knew* and *know*   Ⓓ *retrieve* and *find*

7. Which word from Source 3 is used to emphasize the **suddenness** with which Mr. Tanner's artwork disappeared?

Ⓐ missing   Ⓒ poof

Ⓑ vanished   Ⓓ gone

8. Which of the following quotes from the sources describes something that is easily found if one knows where to look for it?

Ⓐ "pull the missing data out of thin air"   Ⓒ "a split-second decision"

Ⓑ "hiding in plain sight"   Ⓓ "Technology is another story."

Part 3: Search "Into and Out of Thin Air" to find one example each of **synonyms** for the following words. Then write the number of the source in which you located this information.

9. "feeds" _____   Source #: _____

10. "unintentionally" _____   Source #: _____

Name: _____

Part 4: Refer back to the sources, and use complete sentences to answer questions #11 and #13.

11. In Source 3, Mr. Tanner's experience is written in a third-person voice. How might this story be different if it were written in a first-person voice? How would the experience of reading it be different?

_____

_____

_____

_____

12. Imagine that the narrator of Source 4 found the following art file on Mr. Tanner's computer. Use what you have learned to label each stage of the water cycle on the diagram below.

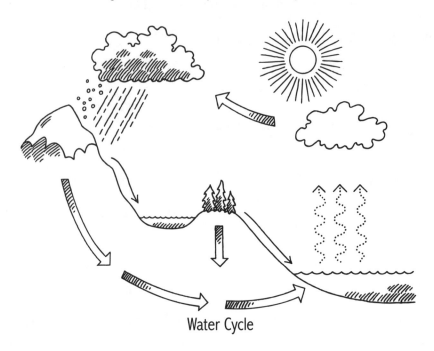

Water Cycle

13. When water is heated, it turns into a gas, evaporates, and rises up to the sky. Does it vanish into thin air? Use the information from the sources to explain your answer.

_____

_____

_____

_____

_____

A Show of Hands and Feet

Read each source below. Then complete the activities on pages 94–95.

Source 1

synecdoche (si-neck-duh-kee)

noun

Definition: a figure of speech in which a part is used to represent a whole or a whole is used to represent a part

Examples:

part representing a whole
— Joe gave us a ride in his new set of <u>wheels</u>." (One part of a car—the wheels—is used to represent the entire car.)

whole representing a part
— Joe said that <u>Germany</u> makes the best cars. (The entire country of *Germany* is used to stand for the few automobile makers in that country.)

Source 2

The words *literal* and *figurative* are antonyms. A literal description describes an event exactly as it happens. A figurative description uses a figure of speech to give an impression about what is happening.

Example: Joe jumped in with both feet.

Literal	Figurative
Joe is literally jumping into a pool of water. Both of his feet are landing in the water.	Joe is trying something new. Instead of slowly and cautiously trying the new thing, Joe is getting involved in it quickly and completely.

Source 3

I heard that Handin Gloves had just changed hands and the new owner was looking for weekend workers to lend them a hand with the transition. I had some time on my hands, so I thought, "Sure, I'll try my hand at warehouse work." Besides, I had recently asked for my girlfriend's hand in marriage, and weddings don't pay for themselves. When I arrived at the company headquarters in Palmville, I announced, "I'm here to lend a hand."

"Sorry," said the new owner, "our work is well in hand. We have enough hired hands to do the job." Just then, however, one of the workers began to complain and misbehave. I was about to warn him that you should never bite the hand that feeds you, but it was too late. The owner fired him and then turned to me and said, "I've got to hand it to you. Your timing is perfect. If you're still interested, the company would like to offer you a position."

As I accepted the job and shook her hand, I said, "You're in good hands."

Source 4

Felicia Foote felt like she had the world at her feet. Things could not be going any better for her. Big Bank of the United States had just handed her a sizable loan, which she used to purchase a company named Handin Gloves. This was Felicia's first venture into the business world, and she was ready to jump in with both feet. For too long, Felicia had relied on her family to foot the bills. She knew it was now time to stand on her own two feet and make her own way. Felicia often threw caution to the wind. She flung herself headfirst into each new endeavor, not worrying about potential problems or setbacks. She felt that she was exceptional at thinking on her feet and solving problems as they arose. Whatever happened, she had always been able to land on her feet.

A Show of Hands and Feet *(cont.)*

Name: _____

Part 1: Read each idea. Which source gives you this information? Fill in the correct bubble for each source. (Note: More than one bubble may be filled in for each idea.)

Information	Sources ➡	1	2	3	4
1. Handin Gloves has changed ownership recently.		○	○	○	○
2. Handin Gloves is now owned by Felicia Foote.		○	○	○	○
3. Handin Gloves is located in Palmville.		○	○	○	○
4. The words *literal* and *figurative* have opposite meanings.		○	○	○	○

Part 2: Fill in the bubble next to the best answer to each question.

5. How is the main character of Source 3 related to the main character of Source 4?

Ⓐ He is a member of her family.

Ⓑ He is her manager.

Ⓒ He is her employee.

Ⓓ He is about to marry her.

6. Which set of words from Source 4 are **not** synonyms?

Ⓐ *potential* and *exceptional*

Ⓑ *venture* and *endeavor*

Ⓒ *threw* and *flung*

Ⓓ *big* and *sizable*

7. Which of the following sentences contains synecdoche?

Ⓐ The parents of the quintuplets had many <u>mouths</u> to feed.

Ⓑ We camped near the <u>mouth</u> of the river.

Ⓒ The librarian <u>mouthed</u> the words, "Be quiet."

Ⓓ Tom was lucky to be born with a silver spoon in his <u>mouth</u>.

8. Writers use *personification* when they give a human quality to a nonhuman object (dog, jacket, house, etc.) or abstract idea (freedom, honesty, etc.). Which of the following phrases uses personification?

Ⓐ "I'm here to lend a hand."

Ⓑ "Weddings don't pay for themselves."

Ⓒ "One of the workers began to complain."

Ⓓ "The new owners were looking for weekend workers."

Part 3: Search "A Show of Hands and Feet" to find one example of each of the following. Then write the number of the source in which you located this information.

9. the name of a European country _____ Source #: _____

10. a compound word with three syllables _____ Source #: _____

Name: _____

Part 4: Refer back to the sources, and use complete sentences to answer these questions.

11. Look at this sentence: Bob the carpenter said, "I can build a table with one arm tied behind my back."

What does this sentence mean if Bob is speaking literally? How about if he is speaking figuratively?

Literally	Figuratively

12. Search Sources 3 and 4 to find three examples of figures of speech that contain synecdoche. Write the quotes in the boxes. On the lines below, choose one quote and explain why it contains synecdoche.

❶

❷

❸

_____

_____

_____

13. Search Sources 3 and 4 to find three examples of figures of speech that **do not** contain synecdoche. Write the quotes in the boxes. On the lines below, choose one quote and explain why it does not contain synecdoche.

❶

❷

❸

_____

_____

_____

The Cookie Question

Read each source below. Then complete the activities on pages 97–99.

Source 1

"It's that time of year again, Grandpa!" announced Amelia. "Want to buy some delicious cookies?"

The elderly man folded his newspaper, removed his reading glasses, and turned toward his granddaughter. "I like cookies."

"That's great, Grandpa. It just so happens that my school is having our annual cookie sale, and if I sell $250 worth of cookies this month, I get a special prize. I've been keeping a sales chart for the first three weeks, and I think I'm going to hit my target goal!"

"That's a lot of cookies! Well, count me in for two boxes of those ones I like."

"You got it, Grandpa! Now which ones did you say you wanted? Do you remember what they looked like or what flavor they were?"

"I just remember the ones I bought last year were so scrumptious."

"I'm going to need more than that, Grandpa. Were they round or square? Did they have peanut butter or mint? There are only five flavors to choose from, so I'm sure we can figure this out."

Grandpa thought for a moment. "They weren't square. What else did you ask? I don't like peanut butter, I can tell you that. Mint? No way." Grandpa made a gesture with this hand to show that he completely dismissed the idea of buying mint cookies.

"Okay, that helps narrow down our choices a bit. Did the cookies have a hole in the middle, or was it a sandwich-type cookie?"

Grandpa slapped his knee excitedly and started to speak before Amelia had stopped. "That's it! I remember feeling like I was getting cheated out of a small morsel of that delectable cookie. Any chance I can get those without holes this year?"

Amelia smiled, "The good news is that I now know which cookie you want. The bad news is that I can't change the way the cookies are made. Sorry!"

Source 2

Adams Elementary Annual Cookie Sale

 Coconut Delights
$4.00 per box

 Fudge Fiestas
$4.50 per box

 Mint Magnificos
$3.50 per box

 Peanut Butter Blasts
$4.00 per box

 Sprinkle Creams
$3.00 per box

Source 3

Amelia's Cookie Sales
Boxes Sold

	Week 1	Week 2	Week 3	Week 4
Coconut Delights	6	1	3	?
Fudge Fiestas	3	3	4	?
Mint Magnificos	5	6	1	?
Peanut Butter Blasts	2	4	5	?
Sprinkle Creams	4	3	7	?
Total	20	17	20	?

The Cookie Question (cont.)

Name: _____

Part 1: Read each idea about Amelia's cookie sale. Which source gives you this information? Fill in the correct bubble for each source. (Note: More than one bubble may be filled in for each idea.)

Information	Sources ➡	1	2	3
1. Some of the cookies being sold contain peanut butter.		○	○	○
2. Some of the cookies being sold contain coconut.		○	○	○
3. Some of the cookies being sold are triangular.		○	○	○
4. Some of the cookies being sold are square.		○	○	○

Part 2: Fill in the bubble next to the best answer to each question.

5. Which of the following words from Source 1 does **not** belong with the others?

   Ⓐ delicious   Ⓒ annual

   Ⓑ delectable   Ⓓ scrumptious

6. Through the first three weeks, of which cookie did Amelia sell the most boxes?

   Ⓐ Fudge Fiestas   Ⓒ Coconut Delights

   Ⓑ Mint Magnificos   Ⓓ Sprinkle Creams

7. In the seventh paragraph of Source 1, Amelia says, "I'm going to need more than that, Grandpa." Of what is she asking for "more"?

   Ⓐ money   Ⓒ information

   Ⓑ cookies   Ⓓ sales

8. Look at these phrases from Source 1. Which of the underlined words is **not** being used as an adverb?

   Ⓐ "The <u>elderly</u> man folded his newspaper"

   Ⓑ "the ones I bought last year were <u>so</u> scrumptious"

   Ⓒ "he <u>completely</u> dismissed the idea"

   Ⓓ "Grandpa slapped his knee <u>excitedly</u>"

Part 3: Search "The Cookie Question" to find one example each of **verbs** with the following meanings. Then write the number of the source in which you located this information.

9. "treated as not worthy of consideration" _____ Source #: _____

10. "to make more limited" _____ Source #: _____

The Cookie Question *(cont.)*

Name: _____

Part 4: Refer back to the sources to answer these questions.

11. Another column has been added to the chart from Source 3. Fill in the column to show how many dollars worth of cookies Amelia has sold through the first three weeks. Then answer the questions below the chart.

	Week 1	Week 2	Week 3	Week 4	$$
Coconut Delights	6	1	3	?	
Fudge Fiestas	3	3	4	?	
Mint Magnificos	5	6	1	?	
Peanut Butter Blasts	2	4	5	?	
Sprinkle Creams	4	3	7	?	
Total	20	17	20	?	

A. How many dollars worth of cookies has she sold so far? _____

B. How many more dollars worth of cookies does she need to sell to meet her target goal? _____

C. How did you find the answer to the previous question (B)?

_____

_____

D. What is the average cost of each box of cookies in the first three weeks? Use the total number of boxes sold and round your answer up to the nearest penny.

_____

E. How did you find the answer to the previous question (D)?

_____

_____

12. Which cookie does Grandpa want to order? Cite evidence from the sources to support your answer.

_____

_____

_____

_____

The Cookie Question *(cont.)*

Name: _____

Part 4 (cont.):

13. **A.** Here are Amelia's sales figures for Week 4 of her contest. Write in the amount of dollars these numbers represent. The first one is done for you.

Cookie	Boxes Sold	$$
Coconut Delights	3	$12
Fudge Fiestas	2	
Mint Magnificos	2	
Peanut Butter Blasts	1	
Sprinkle Creams	4	
Totals	12	

B. Did Amelia meet her goal for the month? Explain.

_____

_____

C. Use the Week 4 figures to complete the bar graph below. The graph has been started for you.

Cookie Boxes Sold ➔ 0	1	2	3	4	5	6	7	8
Coconut Delights								
Week 1								
Week 2								
Week 3								
Week 4								
Fudge Fiestas								
Week 1								
Week 2								
Week 3								
Week 4								
Mint Magnificos								
Week 1								
Week 2								
Week 3								
Week 4								
Peanut Butter Blasts								
Week 1								
Week 2								
Week 3								
Week 4								
Sprinkle Creams								
Week 1								
Week 2								
Week 3								
Week 4								

Additional Activities

1. Now that you have read all of the sources for this unit, do you see any connections between them? What do they have in common? Write up to four connections. (Note: Some units may have fewer.)

_____   _____

_____   _____

Now go back and rank the connections you have just written. Which one seems to be the strongest or most important to the overall unit? Write a "1" next to the strongest connection, a "2" next to the second-strongest, etc.

2. Fill in the chart below to show the elements that describe each source. You may fill in as many bubbles as are appropriate. (Note: Some rows will be left blank if there are fewer than five sources in the unit.)

Source # Element ➡	fiction	nonfiction	chart	map	graph	diagram
Source 1	◯	◯	◯	◯	◯	◯
Source 2	◯	◯	◯	◯	◯	◯
Source 3	◯	◯	◯	◯	◯	◯
Source 4	◯	◯	◯	◯	◯	◯
Source 5	◯	◯	◯	◯	◯	◯

3. It's your turn to be a teacher. Write a new multiple-choice question based on the reading sources. Then provide four answer choices, only one of which is correct. If possible, make your "students" dig a little deeper to find the correct answer to your question. Don't make your question one whose answer is written directly in the text.

Your Question: _____

_____

Ⓐ _____   Ⓒ _____

Ⓑ _____   Ⓓ _____

4. Once again, imagine that you are the teacher. Think of two words, phrases, numbers, etc., that your students will need to search the sources to find. For example, give the definition of a word, and have everyone find that word. Name a part of speech and ask for an example. Challenge your "students" to find a word with a certain number of syllables. There are many possibilities.

Search for _____

Search for _____

Answer Key

Unit 1. Kid in a Candy Store (page 6)

Part 1
1. Paragraph 4
2. Paragraph 2
3. Paragraph 5
4. Paragraph 3

Part 2
5. B   6. B   7. A   8. A

Part 3
The source number is given in parentheses.
9. proceeds (1)   10. connective (2)

Part 4
11. This is figurative language because one could not literally turn closets upside down or inside out. What the narrator is literally doing is going through his/her house thoroughly to find clothing that can be donated for the contest.
12. B. The scale would be needed because candy is sold at Sweet's Sweets by the pound. The cashier would need to weigh the candy to determine how much money the customer owed.
13. Accept appropriate responses that follow the instructions and incorporate at least three similes into the paragraph.

Unit 2. The Plutoed Planet (page 9)

Part 1
1. Sources 1 and 2
2. Source 2
3. Source 3
4. Sources 2 and 3

Part 2
5. A   6. D   7. B   8. C

Part 3
The source number is given in parentheses.
9. ousted (2), stripped (2)   10. journey (1), path (2)

Part 4
11.

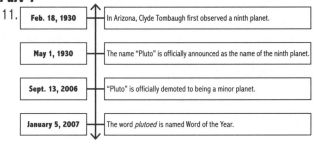

Feb. 18, 1930	In Arizona, Clyde Tombaugh first observed a ninth planet.
May 1, 1930	The name "Pluto" is officially announced as the name of the ninth planet.
Sept. 13, 2006	"Pluto" is officially demoted to being a minor planet.
January 5, 2007	The word *plutoed* is named Word of the Year.

12. Students should mention that Pluto was the name of the god of the cold, dark underworld of mythology. This is appropriate because Pluto would be cold and dark, as it was considered to be the farthest planet from the Sun.
13. Yes, she was alive, as she died in 2009 and Pluto was demoted in 2006. Accept appropriate responses about how students would feel to hear the news of a planet's demotion.

Unit 3. Starting at the Source (page 12)

Part 1
1. Source 3
2. Source 1
3. Sources 1 and 4
4. Source 4

Part 2
5. B and C   6. D   7. B   8. D

Part 3
The source number is given in parentheses.
9. abbreviations (3), exaggeration (4)
10. Minneapolis (1), Louisiana (2, 4)

Part 4
11. Two answers should be circled: "6 years, 1 month" and "73 months." Students should explain that the abbreviation "NB" was first used in October of 1963 and then changed to "NE" in November of 1969. This was a period of time of 6 years and 1 month. Converted to months, this equals a period of 73 months.
12. Accept appropriate responses.
13. In pen, students should do the following: write "MN" and "source" on Minnesota, write "NE" on Nebraska, and write "mouth" on Louisiana. In pencil, they should shade in the following states: Michigan, Florida, Wisconsin, Louisiana, California, New York, Texas, Minnesota, and North Carolina. Below the map, students should write, "The place where a river begins is called its source, and the place where it ends is called its mouth."

Unit 4. The To-Do List (page 16)

Part 1
1. Source 1
2. Sources 1 and 2
3. Sources 1 and 3
4. Source 3

Part 2
5. B   6. C   7. A   8. B

Part 3
The source number is given in parentheses.
9. sleeping like a baby (1)
10. morning's (1), sister's (1)

Part 4
11. A. 40
    B. You need to know how much a quarter is worth (25¢) in order to determine the number of quarters needed to make $10.
12. A. $50
    B. From Source 1, we learn that his mother gave him $60 total. From Source 2, we learn that he spent $9.68 on supplies. That leaves him with a total of $50.32. Rounded to the nearest whole dollar, that amount is $50.
    C. There are a few possible answers. Students should give an answer that satisfies the requirements set forth by the mother in Source 1. For example, $1 bills (15), $5 bills (3), $10 bills (1), quarters (1 roll).
    D. Students should explain that, per the mother's instructions, Jay should get many $1 bills, a few $5 bills, a $10 bill, and one roll of quarters.

Answer Key *(cont.)*

13. Accept appropriate responses. Posters should identify the event ("Garage Sale"), the date (Saturday, July 23, 2016), and some items for sale ("Girls' baby clothes, children's toys, TV set").

Unit 5. The Botched Batch *(page 19)*
Part 1
1. Sources 2 and 3
2. Source 3
3. Sources 2 and 3
4. Source 1

Part 2
5. A
6. B and C
7. A and D
8. C

Part 3
The source number is given in parentheses.
9. separate (2)
10. culinary (4)

Part 4
11. The narrator's cookies looked and tasted awful because of three errors she made while doubling the recipe. First, she did not include enough flour. Two times $2\frac{3}{4}$ equals $5\frac{1}{2}$, but the narrator only used $4\frac{3}{4}$ cups of flour. Next, the narrator forget to double the amount of baking soda the recipe called for. Thirdly, she did double the amount of salt from $\frac{1}{2}$ to 1, but she used a tablespoon instead of a teaspoon.
12. Accept appropriate responses. For example, students might choose the quote, "Trust me, everybody is going to be talking about these cookies after tomorrow." The narrator is implying that people will be talking about the cookies because of how good they are. The irony is that people will be talking about the cookies, but only because of how awful they are.
13. Accept appropriate responses.

Unit 6. Now Hear This *(page 22)*
Part 1
1. Sources 1 and 2
2. Sources 1, 2, and 3
3. Source 2
4. Source 3

Part 2
5. C
6. B
7. B
8. D

Part 3
The source number is given in parentheses.
9. something (1), centerpiece (4), citywide (4)
10. state-of-the-art (4)

Part 4
11. Accept appropriate responses. Students might quote any two sentences from the final paragraph of the article.
12. Accept appropriate responses.
13. Students might point to Mr. Boone's demonstration in Source 1 of a hand cupped behind an ear. A band shell similarly focuses the music in a certain direction (toward the audience). Students might also point to the illustration in Source 4, mentioning that the shell is behind the musicians. This would collect the sound from the instruments and redirect it toward the audience.

Unit 7. Coming In with the Comet *(page 26)*
Part 1
1. Source 2
2. Sources 1, 2, and 4
3. Sources 1 and 2
4. Sources 3 and 4

Part 2
5. C
6. B
7. A
8. B and C

Part 3
The source number is given in parentheses.
9. 1759 (3)
10. *Adventures of Huckleberry Finn* (1)

Part 4
11. Accept appropriate and accurate responses. For the United States, possible answer include:
    A. Declaration of Independence, Revolutionary War, Washington became 1st president, Louisiana Purchase, War of 1812
    B. Lincoln becomes president, Civil War, Ellis Island opens, Spanish-American War, Wright brothers make first flight
    C. World War I, Panama Canal opens, women get right to vote, Great Depression, World War II, Armstrong becomes 1st to walk on the moon, President Nixon resigns
    D. Persian Gulf War, Internet boom, 9/11 terrorist attacks, war against Iraq, Obama becomes 1st African-American president
12. Twain meant that he was born at the time Halley's Comet passed by Earth, and he expected to die around the time it passed by again. In fact, Twain was born exactly two weeks after Halley's Comet was closest to the Sun (in November of 1835), and he died exactly one day after the comet came by again (in April of 1910). Based on the quote given in Source 4, Twain would have been pleased with the timing of his death.
13. Accept appropriate responses.

Unit 8. Dawn of a New Day *(page 29)*
Part 1
1. Sources 1 and 2
2. Sources 2 and 3
3. Source 3
4. Sources 2 and 3

Part 2
5. C
6. B
7. D
8. A and C

Part 3
The source number is given in parentheses.
9. groggily (1)
10. instinctively (1)

Part 4
11. Day of the Week: Saturday. Year: 2009. The day of the week is explicitly stated in Sources 2 and 3, and we are given clues that tell us that both sources take place on the same day (e.g., both say that it is Seth Steven's first day

on the job). We can determine the year from two pieces of information: in Source 3 the narrator says he has owned Hardy's for 37 years, and from Source 1 we know that Hardy's has been owned by the same person since 1972.

12. Personification is used in Source 2 when the author uses pecking birds to represent the thoughts in Seth's mind as he is waking up. The author does this to show that the thoughts are annoying and "attacking" Seth, forcing him to wake up when he would much rather keep sleeping.

13. Accept appropriate responses. Students might say that for Seth Stevens (Source 2), this title describes his new life of having a job. He will no longer have his carefree days of waking up whenever he wants to on the weekend. He now has the responsibility of a new job. For Hal Hardy (Source 3), the title describes his awareness that the business he has built and managed for so long will need to change as he gets older. He will need to find someone to take over for him at some point in the near future.

Unit 9. Drawing Conclusions *(page 32)*
Part 1
1. Source 1
2. Source 4
3. Sources 1 and 4
4. Sources 1 and 3

Part 2
5. D
6. C
7. D
8. C

Part 3
The source number is given in parentheses.
9. rummaged (1)
10. commotion (1)

Part 4
11. Accept appropriate responses. Students might say that Ellie gave the clearest directions. Reasons for this are as follows: the numbered steps are easy to follow, she gives very specific directions, she includes the sizes of certain shapes and distances between shapes, etc.

12. Freddy. Accept appropriate responses in which students answer the question and use at least three temporal words in doing so.

13. Accept appropriate responses. Students should give clear and simple directions for creating the drawing on the page. Students should not mention the end result anywhere in their instructions.

Unit 10. A Silent Start *(page 36)*
Part 1
1. Sources 2 and 3
2. Source 2
3. Source 3
4. Source 1

Part 2
5. C
6. C
7. B
8. D

The 10 words are as follows: Honestly, hour, wrong, knock, knew, write, whole, knows, honor, pseudonym

Part 3
The source number is given in parentheses.
9. rearranging (3)
10. misspell (2)

Part 4
11. "When you think of the word *mnemonic*, think of the word *memory*. Both words have two *m*s in them."

12. Students should rearrange the first letters of the lake names to spell HOMES. Accept appropriate responses for the second part of the question.

13. Accept appropriate responses.

Unit 11. What Is Irrelevant? *(page 39)*
Part 1
1. Source 2
2. Source 3
3. Sources 1 and 2
4. Source 3

Part 2
5. A and D
6. C
7. B
8. B

Part 3
The source number is given in parentheses.
9. insignificant (1), University (3)
10. Greendale's (3), draft's (3), League's (3)

Part 4
11. The first pick was chosen at 12:00 p.m. on Thursday. In Source 3, we learn that Ames was chosen at 3:00 p.m. on Saturday, exactly 51 hours after Kennedy was chosen. You can begin by subtracting 48 hours (2 full days) to get to 3:00 p.m. on Thursday. Subtracting the final 3 hours (48 + 3 = 51) puts the time at 12:00 p.m. on Thursday.

12. Students may suggest word such as *plans*, *attempts*, *looks*, *wants*, *tries*, *strives*, etc. The word *aims* is a good choice by the author because it is homophone for the name of the player about whom the article is written (Drew Ames). Also, *aims* is a short, strong action verb.

13. Accept appropriate responses.

Unit 12. The Chosen Four *(page 42)*
Part 1
1. Sources 1 and 3
2. Source 1
3. Source 1
4. Source 3

Part 2
5. A
6. B
7. D
8. A and D

Part 3
The source number is given in parentheses.
9. shuteye (3)
10. world's (2), nation's (3)

Part 4
11. Answers may vary. The following is a possible rewriting of the entry:

Dear Diary,

I'm so tired. It was a long plane flight back from South Dakota. I visited Mount Rushmore while I was there. It was an absolute thrill and very awe-inspiring. The

Answer Key *(cont.)*

heads were enormous! How did they carve those heads into the face of that mountain? Whoever picked those presidents, chose wisely. Each is so important to our nation's history.

I think Mount Rushmore is on my Mount Rushmore of greatest places I've visited. (Hahaha.) It's right up there with the Grand Canyon, the Golden Gate Bridge, and the Statue of Liberty. Hmm, what do those four have in common? They're gigantic, and they're symbols of America, I suppose.

That's all for now. It's time for some shuteye,
Tess

12. For the final entry, students should write in the current year on the left side of the timeline. For the other entries, students should write in four of the following (in this order): George Washington was president. (1789–1797), Thomas Jefferson was president. (1801–1809), Abraham Lincoln was president. (1861–1865), Theodore Roosevelt was president. (1901–1909), Construction began on Mount Rushmore. (1927), Construction ended on Mount Rushmore. (1941)

13. Accept appropriate responses that follow the directions given.

Unit 13. Even the Odd Ones (page 46)
Part 1
1. Source 1
2. Source 2
3. Sources 2 and 3
4. Sources 2 and 3
Part 2
5. C   6. D   7. C   8. A
Part 3
The source number is given in parentheses.
9. macadamia (3)   10. fork (3)
Part 4
11. We know from the sign on the window in the illustration that *Friend* is the owner's last name, which means that *Friend's* is a possessive proper noun in this case. In the phrase "Audrey's my neighbor," the word *Audrey's* is a contraction for "Audrey" and "is." In the phrase "my neighbor's claims," the word *neighbor's* is possessive but not proper.

12. The narrator does seem to believe Audrey's claims. He knows from experience that she reads a lot and knows a lot of odd information. One quote that illustrates this is, "I knew better than to question one of my neighbor's claims."

13. Answers may vary, but students will probably say that the narrator is the most even of all the characters. The narrator does his best to smooth over any rough spots in the conversation. For example, he interrupts Rick when he's about to challenge Audrey. He does this to diffuse any tension between the two.

Unit 14. Learning the Lingo (page 49)
Part 1
1. Source 3
2. Source 4
3. Source 1
4. Sources 1 and 4
Part 2
5. B   6. C   7. D   8. A
Part 3
The source number is given in parentheses.
9. spectacular (4)   10. generation (4)
Part 4
11. The contranyms are as follows: A. off (first usage means "activated"; second means "deactivated"). B. left (first usage means "departed"; second means "remained"). In either case, students should explain each usage in the context of the sentence.

12. In Source 4, the term "G.O.A.T." is an acronym because each of its letters stands for a whole word. In this case, "G.O.A.T." stands for "Greatest of All Time." This term is also a contranym, because in sports, the term "goat" can mean two very opposite things. In the past, people have called a player a "goat" if he did something wrong that led to the team's defeat. Now, people often call someone a "G.O.A.T." if they are really good. Lastly, "G.O.A.T." is an example of the lingo (or special language) used by a newer generation of sports fans.

13. Accept appropriate responses.

Unit 15. Reaching New Heights (page 52)
Part 1
1. Sources 1 and 4
2. Sources 1 and 4
3. Source 1
4. Source 1
Part 2
5. A and D   6. A   7. C   8. C and D
Part 3
The source number is given in parentheses.
9. consecutive (4)   10. achieve (2), reach (2, 4)
Part 4
11.

#	Name of Building	From	To	Length of Time
1.	Empire State Building	1931	1972	41 years
2.	Sears Tower	1974	1998	24 years
3.	Woolworth Building	1913	1930	17 years
4.	Petronas Towers	1998	2004	6 years
5.	Taipei 101	2004	2010	6 years

12. 4, 1, 3, 5, 2. For the sixth event, possible answer include the following: The world's tallest building was built in Dubai, Suzy Walsham wins her record fifth Run-Up, Maisy O'Day writes an article about the 2014 Run-Up, etc.

13. Accept appropriate responses. Students may state that the title is appropriate to Source 1 because that source is about the new heights that the world's tallest buildings reached over the course of a 100-year span. They may also state that the title is appropriate to athletes such as Suzy Walsham or Thomas Dold who broke and hold records in the Empire State Building Run-Up.

Unit 16. Honoring Olympic Heroes *(page 56)*
Part 1
1. Source 2
2. Sources 2 and 3
3. Sources 1 and 3
4. Source 3

Part 2
5. D   6. B   7. A   8. C

Part 3
The source number is given in parentheses.
9. superior (1)   10. exemplify (3)

Part 4
11. There are several ways to complete the timeline. For example, in the 1900–1950 section, students could add entries for 1936 (Olympic Games held in Berlin; Jesse Owens wins gold medal, etc.) or 1943 (Luz Long dies while fighting in WWII). In the 1950–2000 section, students could add entries for 1964 (Luz Long awarded Pierre de Coubertin Medal) or 1988 (Lawrence Lemieux awarded Pierre de Coubertin Medal).

12. Accept appropriate responses. Students should provide ways in which the two athletes are similar (both showed courage; both put sportsmanship above winning, etc.) and ways they are different (Long came in 2nd, while Lemieux came in 22nd; Lemieux was alive when he received the de Coubertin medal, Long was not, etc.).

13. Accept appropriate responses that use the first-person voice to give an account of the experience from the perspective of either Owens or Long.

Unit 17. A Storm with Your Name *(page 59)*
Part 1
1. Source 2
2. Sources 2, 3, and 4
3. Sources 2 and 4
4. Source 1

Part 2
5. B   6. B   7. C   8. B

Part 3
9. particularly   10. hole, whole

Part 4
11. chronological order: Charley, Frances, Ivan, Jeanne, Katrina, Rita, Wilma, Ike, Irene, Sandy. Even though we are only given the years in which these hurricanes occurred, we can still put them in chronological order. This is because we know from Source 2 that within each year, hurricanes are named in alphabetical order. Therefore, we know, for example, that

Hurricane Charley came first because "C" comes before "F" (Frances), "I" (Ivan), or "J" (Jeanne) in the alphabet.

12. Students might observe that wind speed doesn't necessarily equate to costlier or deadlier hurricanes. For example, Jeanne was a Category 3 hurricane but it was much deadlier than Category 5 storms like Wilma and Rita. Sandy was another Category 3 storm, and it was much costlier than some stronger hurricanes. Students might also point out that a large percentage of these hurricanes occurred in 2004 and 2005.

13. Accept appropriate responses that are written in the first-person voice.

Unit 18. About Alike Animals *(page 62)*
Part 1
1. Source 2
2. Sources 1 and 3
3. Source 4
4. Sources 3 and 4

Part 2
5. D   6. C   7. C   8. C

Part 3
The source number is given in parentheses.
9. eager (1)   10. squinted (3)

Part 4
11. You would never find all <u>of these animals</u> in one place <u>at the same time</u>.

12. Students will most likely say that Julie is like Misha. Both examine things closely and take things very seriously (according to their friends, at least).

13. Possible answers include the following: The monkey is <u>in the tree</u>. The ape is <u>beside the tree</u>. The crocodile is <u>in the river</u>. The frog is <u>on the lily pad</u>. The turtle is <u>near the water</u>.

Unit 19. We Can All Agree *(page 66)*
Part 1
1. both movies
2. *Moose on Mars III*
3. *Moose on Mars III*
4. *The Tails of Two Kitties*

Part 2
5. B   6. A   7. B   8. B

Part 3
The source number is given in parentheses.
9. hilarious (3)   10. concern (1)

Part 4
11.

	The Tails of Two Kitties	**Moose on Mars III**
Start Time	2:30	3:00
Running Time	123 minutes	77 minutes
Ending Time	4:33	4:17

12. Penny agrees to see the movie because it contains animal characters. Brian agrees to see it because it has a science-fiction element (Mars) to it and because he has

liked the other movies in the series. Dad agrees to see it because it will end in time for him to get dinner started.

13. Accept appropriate responses.

Unit 20. A Way Across (page 69)
Part 1
1. Sources 2 and 3
2. Source 2
3. Sources 2 and 3
4. Source 3

Part 2
5. A
6. C
7. A and C
8. B, C, and D

Part 3
The source number is given in parentheses.
9. 1830s (4)
10. telegraph operator (3)

Part 4
11. Accept appropriate responses. Students should mention how the telegraph allowed a way for communication to travel quickly across great distances, just as the transcontinental railroad provided a way for people and goods to travel much farther and much more quickly.

12. Accept appropriate responses. Students might write about how the narrator felt that the United States was greater because it was now a more advanced country with the means to travel quickly from coast to coast. This route also made the country smaller in that travel across the land could now be done in a much shorter time frame.

13. Accept appropriate responses. Students might discuss how people back then were interested and excited to quickly get news of recent events, just as they are today. To contrast the means of communication available back then with those available now, students might discuss how news is spread these days (via the Internet, etc.) and how images (videos) and messages of all lengths are transmitted immediately.

Unit 21. Words Made from Myths (page 72)
Part 1
1. Sources 1 and 3
2. Sources 1 and 2
3. Source 1
4. Sources 1 and 4

Part 2
5. C
6. B and C
7. C
8. A and D

Part 3
The source number is given in parentheses.
9. receded (1)
10. vicious (1)

Part 4
11. In Source 4, the word *Sisyphean* is used as an allusion. It is mentioned briefly, and readers are expected to know the meaning behind this word. They are expected to know that the author is saying that hunting at night for insects would be impossible for humans. The word *echo* is never used as an allusion in Source 4. It is simply used to describe the science of sound waves bouncing off of objects. The Greek figure Echo is never mentioned or alluded to.

12. Accept appropriate responses. For example, the first panel might show Sisyphus pushing a rock up a hill and saying something like, "Maybe this will be the time I get this rock up to the top." The second panel might show Sisyphus near the top, saying something like, "I knew I could it!" The third panel would show the rock rolling back down the hill. Looking dejected, Sisyphus would be saying something like, "No, not again!"

13. Accept appropriate responses.

Unit 22. Which "Sound" Do You See? (page 76)
Part 1
1. Source 4
2. Source 2
3. Source 1
4. Source 3

Part 2
5. C
6. B
7. B
8. D

Part 3
The source number is given in parentheses.
9. ceased (5)
10. ominous (5)

Part 4
11. A. noun, 1
B. verb, 1
C. noun, 1
D. noun, 2
E. verb, 2
F. adjective, 2
G. adjective, 3
H. adjective, 1
I. adverb, 1

12. Accept appropriate responses. Students may say that the troop is large, and as evidence, they may state that the troop leader always seems to be shouting or hollering, even when the soldiers are quiet.

13. Accept appropriate responses.

Unit 23. What's in a Name? (page 79)
Part 1
1. Sources 2 and 3
2. Source 2
3. Source 3
4. Sources 1 and 2

Part 2
5. B
6. C
7. A
8. B and D

Part 3
The source number is given in parentheses.
9. today's, kiwi's, country's (3)
10. New Zealand's (2)

Part 4
11. "Kimi would not touch that plate with a ten-foot pole."

12. C (ostriches); This analogy is comparing the sizes of things. Ostriches (larger bird) are to kiwis (smaller bird) as kiwi eggs (larger in size) are to chicken eggs (smaller in size).

13. Accept appropriate responses that follow the instructions and retell an event from Source 1 from the perspective of the Kimi who comes from Kentucky and is a vegetarian.

Unit 24. When You're From (page 82)
Part 1
1. Sources 1 and 3
2. Sources 1, 2, and 4
3. Sources 1 and 2
4. Source 2

Answer Key *(cont.)*

Part 2

5. D   6. B   7. C   8. C

Part 3

The source number is given in parentheses.

9. alphabetically (4)   10. grasp (1)

Part 4

11. A. 50% of the scientists listed were born in the 19ᵗʰ century. B. Four of the eight scientists listed were born in the 1800s, which means that half (or 50%) were born in the 19th century. C. In chronological order, those scientists are Charles Darwin (born 1809), Louis Pasteur (born 1822), Marie Curie (born 1867), and Albert Einstein (born 1879).

12. Answers will vary. Students can point to many clues that tell us that Source 1 is a work of fiction. The play is about time travel, the main character has a conversation with a historical figure, and a great mathematician like Isaac Newton would most likely not be so eager to hear the narrator's math trick for determining a person's birthday.

13. Answers will vary. In the first answer, students should demonstrate their understanding of the material from Source 3. Each student's answer should be a five- or six-digit number, depending on his/her birth month.

Unit 25. Teaching the New Teacher *(page 86)*

Part 1

1. Sources 1 and 3   3. Source 1
2. Sources 1 and 2   4. Source 3

Part 2

5. C   6. A   7. B   8. C

Part 3

The source number is given in parentheses.

9. complement (1)   10. compliment (1)

Part 4

11. Students should draw two symbols in the 2006 column (Quinton and Pamela), five in the 2007 column (Jenny, Jace, Willow, Allison, and Andrew), and three in the 2008 column (Gaby, Ceci, and Daniel).

12. Answers will vary. The following needs should be reflected in the chart: Ceci should sit near the door, Pamela should sit near the window, Jace should sit near the front of the class, and Jenny and Willow should be seated on opposite sides of the classroom.

13. Answers might vary. Possible answers are as follows: Kinesthetic: Jenny or Willow; "You'll see them jumping rope together or practicing gymnastics every day at recess." Linguistic: Daniel; "Daniel is a little more reserved, but he's an excellent writer." Naturalist: Pamela; "She likes looking at the trees swaying in the breeze, and it seems to help her think more clearly."

Unit 26. Into and Out of Thin Air *(page 90)*

Part 1

1. Sources 2 and 3   3. Sources 2 and 4
2. Source 2   4. Source 3

Part 2

5. D   6. C   7. C   8. B

Part 3

The source number is given in parentheses.

9. nourishes (2)   10. accidentally (4)

Part 4

11. Accept appropriate responses.

12.

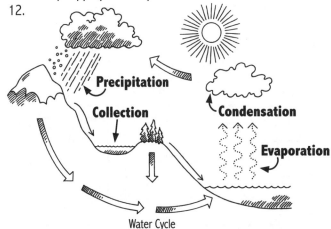

Water Cycle

13. Accept appropriate answers. Students should say that the water doesn't vanish into thin air. If it vanished into thin air, the water would disappear completely, never to return. That is not how the water cycle works. Instead, the water eventually cools down, returns to liquid form, and becomes clouds.

Unit 27. A Show of Hands and Feet *(page 93)*

Part 1

1. Sources 3 and 4   3. Source 3
2. Source 4   4. Source 2

Part 2

5. C   6. A   7. A   8. B

Part 3

The source number is given in parentheses.

9. Germany (1)   10. headquarters (3)

Part 4

11. *Literally:* This would mean that Bob feels he could build a table even if one of his arms is really tied behind his back. *Figuratively:* This would mean that Bob feels he is such an expert carpenter that building a table is very easy for him. He could even do it if he had a difficult obstacle to overcome.

12. There are several possibilities to choose from, especially involving the word *hand* in Source 3. In most cases, students need to show how the word *hand* is used to represent a whole person. For example, the term "hired hands" is used to represent whole people who have been hired to work.

13. There are several possibilities to choose from, especially involving the word *feet* in Source 4. Students need to show how the word is used figuratively, but does not represent a larger whole (as would be the case with synecdoche). For example, the phrase "stand on my own two feet" means that the person is not relying on others for help.

Unit 28. The Cookie Question *(page 96)*

Part 1

1. Sources 1, 2, and 3
2. Sources 2 and 3
3. Source 2
4. Sources 1 and 2

Part 2

5. C
6. D
7. C
8. A

Part 3

The source number is given in parentheses.

9. dismissed (1)
10. narrow (1)

Part 4

11.

Cookie	Week 1	Week 2	Week 3	Week 4	$$
Coconut Delights	6	1	3	?	$40
Fudge Fiestas	3	3	4	?	$45
Mint Magnificos	5	6	1	?	$42
Peanut Butter Blasts	2	4	5	?	$44
Sprinkle Creams	4	3	7	?	$42
Total	20	17	20	?	

A. $213

B. $37

C. In Source 1, Amelia says that her target goal is $250. $250 − $213 = $37

D. $3.74

E. According to the chart, Amelia has sold 57 boxes of cookies so far. Together, these boxes have cost $213. $213 ÷ 57 = $3.74.

12. Grandpa wants the Sprinkle Creams. We know from his conversation with Amelia that the cookies he wants are not square, and they do not contain mint or peanut butter. We know that they have a hole in them. The only cookies that fit all of these criteria are the Sprinkle Creams.

13. A.

Cookie	Boxes Sold	$$
Coconut Delights	3	$12
Fudge Fiestas	2	$9
Mint Magnificos	2	$7
Peanut Butter Blasts	1	$4
Sprinkle Creams	4	$12
Totals	12	$44

B. Yes, her total sales figures added up to $257, so she exceeded her goal by $7.

C.

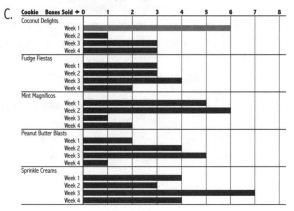

Common Core State Standards

The lessons and activities included in *Mastering Complex Text Using Multiple Reading Sources, Grade 4* meet the following Common Core State Standards. (©Copyright 2010. National Governors Association Center for Best Practices and Council of Chief State School Officers. All rights reserved.) For more information about the Common Core State Standards, go to *http://www.corestandards.org/* or visit *http://www.teachercreated.com/standards/* for more correlations to Common Core State Standards.

Reading: Informational Text	
Key Ideas and Details	**Units**
ELA.RI.4.1 Refer to details and examples in a text when explaining what the text says explicitly and when drawing inferences from the text.	1–28
ELA.RI.4.2 Determine the main idea of a text and explain how it is supported by key details; summarize the text.	5–7, 11, 14–15, 19–20, 23–24, 26, 28
ELA.RI.4.3 Explain events, procedures, ideas, or concepts in a historical, scientific, or technical text, including what happened and why, based on specific information in the text.	2, 5–7, 12, 16–17, 19–20, 23–24, 26
Craft and Structure	**Units**
ELA.RI.4.4 Determine the meaning of general academic and domain-specific words or phrases in a text relevant to a *grade 4 topic or subject area.*	1–28
ELA.RI.4.5 Describe the overall structure (e.g., chronology, comparison, cause/effect, problem/solution) of events, ideas, concepts, or information in a text or part of a text.	4–5, 7–9, 12, 14–16, 19–20, 23, 25–26
ELA.RI.4.6 Compare and contrast a firsthand and secondhand account of the same event or topic; describe the differences in focus and the information provided.	10, 17, 20, 26
Integration of Knowledge and Ideas	**Units**
ELA.RI.4.7 Interpret information presented visually, orally, or quantitatively (e.g., in charts, graphs, diagrams, time lines, animations, or interactive elements on Web pages) and explain how the information contributes to an understanding of the text in which it appears.	3–4, 6–7, 9–10, 12, 15, 17–19, 23, 25–26, 28
ELA.RI.4.8 Explain how an author uses reasons and evidence to support particular points in a text.	1–28
ELA.RI.4.9 Integrate information from two texts on the same topic in order to write or speak about the subject knowledgeably.	1–28

Common Core State Standards *(cont.)*

Reading: Informational Text *(cont.)*	
Range of Reading and Level of Text Complexity	**Units**
ELA.RI.4.10 By the end of the year, read and comprehend informational texts, including history/social studies, science, and technical texts, in the grades 4—5 text complexity band proficiently, with scaffolding as needed at the high end of the range.	1–28
Reading: Literature	
Key Ideas and Details	**Units**
ELA.RL.4.1 Refer to details and examples in a text when explaining what the text says explicitly and when drawing inferences from the text.	1–28
ELA.RL.4.2 Determine a theme of a story, drama, or poem from details in the text; summarize the text.	6–8, 13, 20, 24
ELA.RL.4.3 Describe in depth a character, setting, or event in a story or drama, drawing on specific details in the text (e.g., a character's thoughts, words, or actions).	5, 7–8, 10, 13, 15, 18–20, 23–24, 26
Craft and Structure	**Units**
ELA.RL.4.4 Determine the meaning of words and phrases as they are used in a text, including those that allude to significant characters found in mythology (e.g., Herculean).	1–28
ELA.RL.4.5 Explain major differences between poems, drama, and prose, and refer to the structural elements of poems (e.g., verse, rhythm, meter) and drama (e.g., casts of characters, settings, descriptions, dialogue, stage directions) when writing or speaking about a text.	24
ELA.RL.4.6 Compare and contrast the point of view from which different stories are narrated, including the difference between first- and third-person narrations.	8–10, 17, 20, 26
Range of Reading and Level of Text Complexity	**Units**
ELA.RL.4.10 By the end of the year, read and comprehend literature, including stories, dramas, and poetry, in the grades 4—5 text complexity band proficiently, with scaffolding as needed at the high end of the range.	1–28
Reading: Foundational Skills	
Phonics and Word Recognition	**Units**
ELA.RF.4.3 Know and apply grade-level phonics and word-analysis skills in decoding words.	1–28
Fluency	**Units**
ELA.RF.4.4 Read with sufficient accuracy and fluency to support comprehension.	1–28

Common Core State Standards (cont.)

Writing	
Text Types and Purposes	**Units**
ELA.W.4.1 Write opinion pieces on topics or texts, supporting a point of view with reasons and information.	1–28
ELA.W.4.1A Introduce a topic or text clearly, state an opinion, and create an organizational structure in which related ideas are grouped to support the writer's purpose.	1–28
ELA.W.4.1B Provide reasons that are supported by facts and details.	1–28
ELA.W.4.1C Link opinion and reasons using words and phrases (e.g., *for instance*, *in order to*, *in addition*).	1–28
ELA.W.4.2 Write informative/explanatory texts to examine a topic and convey ideas and information clearly.	1–28
ELA.W.4.2B Develop the topic with facts, definitions, concrete details, quotations, or other information and examples related to the topic.	1–28
ELA.W.4.2C Link ideas within categories of information using words and phrases (e.g., *another*, *for example*, *also*, *because*).	1–28
ELA.W.4.2D Use precise language and domain-specific vocabulary to inform about or explain the topic.	1–28
ELA.W.4.3 Write narratives to develop real or imagined experiences or events using effective technique, descriptive details, and clear event sequences.	1–2, 5–10, 14, 16–17, 19, 23, 26
Production and Distribution of Writing	**Units**
ELA.W.4.4 Produce clear and coherent writing in which the development and organization are appropriate to task, purpose, and audience.	1–28
Research to Build and Present Knowledge	**Units**
ELA.W.4.8 Recall relevant information from experiences or gather relevant information from print and digital sources; take notes and categorize information, and provide a list of sources.	1–28
ELA.W.4.9 Draw evidence from literary or informational texts to support analysis, reflection, and research.	1–28
Range of Writing	**Units**
ELA.W.4.10 Write routinely over extended time frames (time for research, reflection, and revision) and shorter time frames (a single sitting or a day or two) for a range of discipline-specific tasks, purposes, and audiences.	1–28

Common Core State Standards *(cont.)*

Language	
Conventions of Standard English	**Units**
ELA.L.4.1 Demonstrate command of the conventions of standard English grammar and usage when writing or speaking.	1–28
ELA.L.4.2 Demonstrate command of the conventions of standard English capitalization, punctuation, and spelling when writing.	1–28
Knowledge of Language	**Units**
ELA.L.4.3 Use knowledge of language and its conventions when writing, speaking, reading, or listening.	1–28
Vocabulary Acquisition and Use	**Units**
ELA.L.4.4 Determine or clarify the meaning of unknown and multiple-meaning words and phrases based on grade 4 reading and content, choosing flexibly from a range of strategies.	1–28
ELA.L.4.4A Use context (e.g., definitions, examples, or restatements in text) as a clue to the meaning of a word or phrase.	1–28
ELA.L.4.4B Use common, grade-appropriate Greek and Latin affixes and roots as clues to the meaning of a word (e.g., *telegraph, photograph, autograph*).	7, 10–11, 14, 20–21
ELA.L.4.5 Demonstrate understanding of figurative language, word relationships, and nuances in word meanings.	1–28
ELA.L.4.5A Explain the meaning of simple similes and metaphors (e.g., *as pretty as a picture*) in context.	1, 4, 8, 20, 27
ELA.L.4.5B Recognize and explain the meaning of common idioms, adages, and proverbs.	1, 4–5, 7–8, 12–16, 18, 23, 27
ELA.L.4.5C Demonstrate understanding of words by relating them to their opposites (antonyms) and to words with similar but not identical meanings (synonyms).	1–2, 5–16, 19–20, 22–24, 26, 28
ELA.L.4.6 Acquire and use accurately grade-appropriate general academic and domain-specific words and phrases, including those that signal precise actions, emotions, or states of being (e.g., *quizzed, whined, stammered*) and that are basic to a particular topic (e.g., *wildlife, conservation,* and *endangered* when discussing animal preservation).	1–28